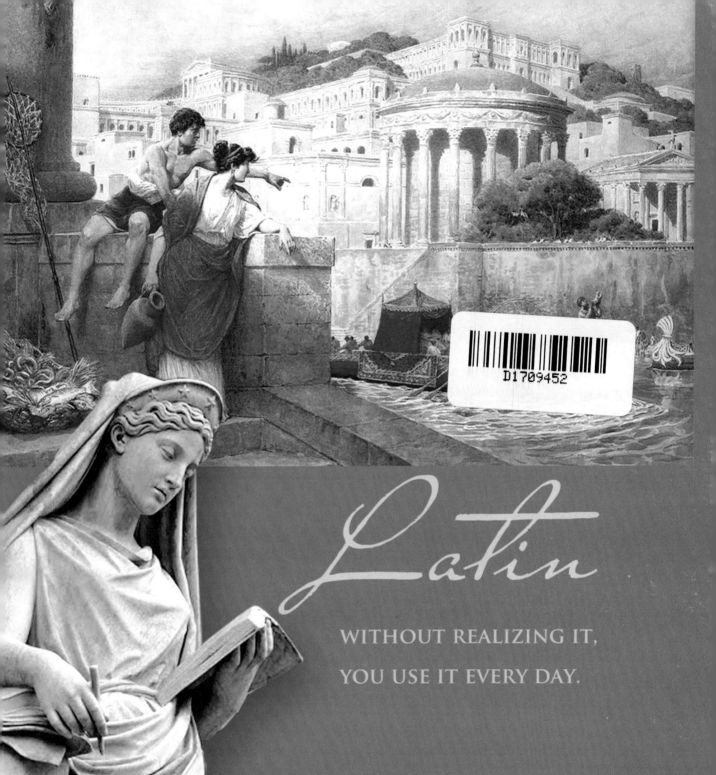

Latin

WITHOUT REALIZING IT,

YOU USE IT EVERY DAY.

Hi, my Latin name is *Flavia*. You can call me *Magistra Flavia*. I will be your teacher in this beginner Latin course for kids. I will teach you *Lingua Latina*!

magistra – female teacher • *lingua* – language • *Latina* – Latin (an adjective)

It would be great if you took a Latin name too – read about Latin names at the end of this chapter! ...Uh-oh!

Well, there is a grain of truth here: Around AD 300 the citizens of the Roman Empire had 200 holidays – days off work! Why are we not surprised that Rome lost its power and glory, and was destroyed by barbarians? To work, kids! We don't want this to happen to us, do we?

Latin Pronunciation

There are two ways of pronouncing Latin words:

Classical Latin (from ancient Rome – *Roma antiqua*) and

Ecclesiastical Latin (Church, or Medieval Latin.) We'll use the Classical pronunciation.

Classical Latin pronunciation

c - as in cat

g - as in garden

a - as in father

e - as in net

i - as in machine

o - as in hot

u - as in rude

y - as i

ae - as in eye

au - as in mouse

eu - as e- (as in pet) -u (as in put)

oe - as in foil

qu - as kw

Stress

In Latin, the stress falls on either the second or the third syllable from the end of the word. In the days of Ancient Rome some vowels in Latin were short and some were long. If the second syllable from the end had a long vowel, that syllable was stressed. When I introduce a multi-syllable word, I will mark the stressed syllable with a dot like this – *Salvete!*

> LATIN IS HARD? SO WHAT? A CHALLENGE ENDS IN A DEFEAT ONLY WHEN YOU DON'T TRY.

VIR FORTIS

ARMA

INSCRIPTIO

LAPIDES

TERRA ROMANA

FLOS

PAPILIO

LESSON I

About 60 percent of all English words come from Latin. Whenever we learn new Latin words, I will list modern English words related to them. These English words will be highlighted in yellow.

How do you say 'Hello!' in Latin?
You can say: *Salve!*
Salve is a form of the Latin verb
salvere – to save
It's like saying 'God save you.'
Your response to *Salve!* can be
Salve et tu! – And hello to you!

salve – hello – salvation

Latin goodbye is *Vale!*- a form of the Latin verb
valere – to be well, to be strong – valid, validity
Your response to *Vale!* can be
Vale et tu! = And goodbye to you!

DUM SPIRO, SPERO.

WHILE I BREATHE, I HOPE.

ACTA NON VERBA

ACTIONS NOT WORDS

Here is some good news about Latin: In Latin there are no articles – *a, an, the*!
One thing less to worry about!

Ancient Romans used a metal pen called a *stylus* to write on panels of wood covered with wax. The top end of the pen had a flat eraser to smooth out mistakes in the wax.

To ask in Latin 'What is this?' you would say:
Quid est?
Quid – what
est – is
Quid est? Liber.
Quid est? Stylus.

to be – esse; *est* = it is, he is, she is
liber – book – library
stylus – pen – style, stylish

Please ask in Latin, "What is this?" and answer using words:
stylus, tabula, liber, aqua
To ask 'Who is this?' you would say:
Quis est? (about a man)
Quae est? (about a woman)
Quae est Flavia? Flavia magistra est.
Quis est Iulius? Iulius discipulus est.

tabula – Roman wax tablet for making notes   table
aqua – water – aquarium, aquatic, aquamarine
discipulus / discipula – student – disciple, discipline

Have you ever seen the abbreviation *i.e.*? It stands for *id est* – 'that is.'

Writers use this expression to say 'which means,' 'that is to say,' or 'in other words.'

For example, you can write: I am studying *Lingua Latina*, i.e. Latin language.

Now, what is *est*? It's a form of the Latin verb *esse* – to be.

GRAMMAR: Verb *esse*

Verbs with the meaning *to be* are some of the oldest and most frequently used words in most

languages. And because they are so ancient, they are usually a little crazy. Take a look at

the English verb *to be*. We say *I am*, but *you are*, and *he is*! Am, is, are – are all forms

of the verb *to be*! When a verb changes its form we call it *conjugation*.

While English verb *to be* has 3 different forms in present tense – *am, is, are* –

Latin verbs have 6 different forms! I know, it's a lot to handle, but don't panic (yet)!

Trust me, there is good news down the road! So stay with me, and let's conjugate

the Latin verb *esse* – to be.

English word pen comes from
Latin *penna* – a feather, a quill

I am – *sum*

you are – *es*

he/she/it is – *est*

we are – *sumus*

you (more than 1 person) are – *estis*

they are – *sunt*

English word *interesting* comes from the Latin verb
interesse – to be between, to take part in, to be important
interesse = *inter* (between) + *esse* (to be)
Interest means 'He/she/it is important.'

When I learn Latin verbs, I write

7 forms for each verb like this:

esse

sum – es – est

sumus – estis – sunt

The promised good news is,

when you use Latin verbs, you can totally drop any pronouns!

It's as if instead of saying *I am*, you just say *am*.

Am is used only with *I*, so why even bother to use *I*?

That's precisely what Romans did.

Sum is *I am* – you don't need any pronoun!

Magistra sum. – I am a teacher.

So I am just saying *Am teacher*. Easy, right?

MONSTRUM SUM.

QUIS ES?

SERPENS MAGNUS SUM!

SERPENS TERRIBILIS SUM!

SH-H-H-H! SERPENTES STUPIDI ESTIS! MAGISTRAM AUDITE!

To ask a question Romans often used the suffix *ne*, attaching it to a word in their question:

Es + ne >> Esne discipulus? Esne discipula? Are you a student?

Est + ne >> Estne magistra? Is she a teacher?

> *MINIME! DISCIPULUS NON SUM. INSECTUM SUM.*

Romans had no words for 'yes' or 'no.' Instead, they simply repeated the question as an affirmative or negative statement: 'Are you a teacher?' – 'I am a teacher' or 'I am not a teacher.' Romans also used these words in place of 'yes':

ita – so

ita vero – so indeed

ita est – it is so

certe – certainly

sic – so, this way

> *ITA VERO, MONSTRUM MAGNUM ET TERRIBILE SUM!*

Esne magistra?
Ita, magistra sum.

Esne discipulus / discipula?
Please answer
'Yes, I am a student' in Latin.

> *MINIME! STUPIDUM NON SUM!*

> *MONSTRUM INTELLEGENS SUM.*

To say 'no,'
Romans also used:

non – no, not

minime – no, unlikely

minime vero – not true

To answer a question negatively, use *non*:

Non sum magister. Sum discipulus.
Non sum magistra. Sum discipula.

By the way, 'and' in Latin is *et*

liber et stylus – book and pen

silva et domus – forest and house

dominus et magister – lord and teacher

magister et discipulus – teacher and student

dominus et domina – lord and lady

> *VALE, AMICI!*

Proverbia et Dicta (Proverbs & Sayings)

In every lesson we'll learn 2-3 Latin expressions or phrases – from either Classical Latin or from Church Latin. The English word 'proverb' comes from Latin *pro* = forth and *verbum* = word

1. *Natura, artis magistra* –
Nature is the teacher of the arts

2. *Anno Domini* – In the year of our Lord – or, as an abbreviation, *AD*. As you know, *AD* is used to indicate the years after the birth of Jesus Christ. For example 'AD 2020.'

silva – forest

domus – house – domestic

dominus – lord, Mr. – dominion, dominate

domina – lady, Mrs. – dame

3. In English we use the Latin expression *et cetera* which means 'and so on.' Usually it is written as an abbreviation *etc*. *Cetera* means 'the rest' in Latin.

et cetera – and the rest... and so on

People who don't know Latin often mispronounce 'et cetera' as 'ek cetera.' But as a student of Latin, you won't make this mistake!

abbreviation – comes from the Latin word
brevis - short – brevity

GRAMMAR: Latin Nouns - Number and Gender

POCULUM POTIONIS SINENSIS

Like English nouns, Latin nouns have a plural and a singular form, for example:

magister – teacher >> *magistri* – teachers

discipulus – student >> *discipuli* – students

Also, Latin nouns have a gender. A noun can be masculine, feminine, or neuter. You can tell that
magister and *discipulus* are masculine nouns. We use them when speaking of a man or a boy.
Magistra and *discipula* are feminine nouns – used when speaking of a woman or a girl.
But things are not all that simple in Latin! Every single noun in Latin has a gender –
even words like 'pen,' 'table,' 'water,' etc.

Silva (forest) and *aqua* (water) are feminine,
but *stylus* (pen) and *liber* (book) are masculine!
And *monstrum* (monster) and *animal* (animal)
are neuter! Why on earth??? Nobody knows!

monstrum n. – monster

animal n. – animal

Fortunately, you can often tell the gender of a noun by its ending:

masculine nouns often end in *-us* like *discipulus, dominus, or octopus*
or in *-r, -er, -ir* like *magister*.

Feminine nouns often end in *-a* like
magistra, discipula, or *fortuna* (fortune.)

Many neuter nouns end in *-um*, like
solarium – sundial, *argentum* – silver, *aurum* – gold

aurum n. – gold

argentum n. – silver,
money – Argentina

templum n. – temple

solarium n. – sundial

Whenever I introduce a new noun I'll add
these abbreviations to indicate its gender:

m. – masculine, *f.* – feminine, *n.* – neuter

indicate comes from the Latin word
indicare – to point out – It's the
same root as in 'index finger')

Masculine nouns ending in *-us, -r, -er, -ir* end in *-i* in the plural

discipulus – *discipuli* • *magister* – *magistri* • *liber* – *libri*

Feminine nouns ending in *-a* end in *-ae* in the plural

magistra – *magistrae* • *domina* – *dominae* • *silva* – *silvae*

Neuter nouns ending in *-um* end in *-a* in the plural

solarium – *solaria* • *templum* – *templa*

The mother walrus lectures to the
baby walrus: "You shouldn't be
selfish! Always think of others.
After all it's *walr-US*, not
walr-I." Baby walrus is puzzled:
"My Latin teacher says the *- us*
ending is singular, and the *- i*
ending is plural."

HOMEWORK

Please translate these sentences and phrases from English to Latin:

Are you a teacher? I am not a teacher. I am a student.

What is this? This is a book. Is this a pen? This is a pen.

Isn't this silver? This is not silver. It's gold.

Are you students? We are students (male or female).

Are they teachers? They are teachers (male or female).

Are you teachers and students? We are not teachers, we are students.

forests and languages • temples and markets (*mercatum* n.)

silver and gold • pens and books • lords and ladies

Is this a house? No, it's not a house. It's a temple.

The correct answers are at the end of the book,
but don't you dare look there until you finish
writing your own answers in nice, clear handwriting.

HMMMM…
HOMO NON SUM.
EQUUS NON SUM,
QUIS SUM?

Reading – Schola

CENTAURUS ES!

Haec est Cornelia. Quae est Cornelia? Estne Cornelia femina?

Non femina, sed puella est Cornelia. Estne Cornelia magistra?

Non magistra, sed discipula Cornelia est. Flavia est femina.

Flavia est magistra. Flavia dicit: "Salve, Cornelia! Esne discipula?"

Cornelia respondet: "Salve, Magistra! Ita, discipula sum."

Magistra dicit: "Quid est?"

Cornelia respondet:"Stylus."

Magistra dicit: "Quid est?"

Cornelia respondet:"Tabula."

Magistra dicit: "Quid est?"

Cornelia respondet: "Nescio."

Magistra dicit: "Hoc solarium est."

hoc, haec – this • *puella f.* – girl
nescio – I don't know • *sed* – but
dicit – says, *dicere* – to say
respondet – answers

Who are Valedictorian and Salutatorian?

When a person graduates from school at the top
of their class, that person is called the *valedictorian*.
Valedictorian comes from two Latin roots
vale – 'good bye' and *dicere* – 'say.'
That's right, the *valedictorian* is the person who gives
the final – or the good-bye – speech at the graduation
ceremony – a huge honor! The student who is
the next best student after the *Valedictorian*
in the graduating class is called the *Salutatorian*,
after the Latin word *salutare* – to say 'hello.'
That's because the *Salutatorian* is usually the first
to make a speech at the graduation ceremony.

LATIN NAMES

Coccinella septempunctata Linnaeus sum.

Roman men had 3 names: *praenomen* – a personal name used only by the members of the family,
nomen – family name, and *cognomen* – a nickname.
Examples: **Gaius Julius Caesar, Marcus Flavius Valerius Constantinus**

Roman women had only *nomen* – the feminine form of the family name and *cognomen* – nickname.
If Julius, a man from the Julii family, had 3 daughters, they would all be called Julia with different
cognomens/nicknames, like Julia *Major* – Big Julia (eldest daughter), Julia *Minor* – Little Julia
(youngest daughter), Julia *Secunda* (Second Julia), Julia *Tertia* (Third Julia), and so on.
If the father had a memorable or honorable cognomen, his daughters often added it to their name
as well. For example, Roman general **Publius Cornelius Scipio Africanus** received his honorary
cognomen *Africanus* after his military victories in North Africa. His daughter Cornelia
was known as **Cornelia Africana.**

So, if you are a boy, use the lists below to come up with a 3-part name for yourself – Roman style!
If you are a girl, use a female form of a nomen, and if you have a sister, use a cognomen
Major, Minor, Secunda, Tertia, Quarta. Also, in the late days of the Roman Empire women started
using additional cognomens/nicknames, so grab yourself one from the list below, or come up with
one! For example, my full Latin name is **Flavia Marina • Marina** = of the sea

Apis mellifera Linnaeus sum.

Praenomen – male only:

Marcus, Gaius, Publius, Lucius, Titus, Aulus, Decimus, Quintus

Nomen – male and female :

Claudius – Claudia, Lemonius – Lemonia, Flavius – Flavia, Julius – Julia, Cornelius – Cornelia,
Aurelius – Aurelia, Aemilius – Aemilia, Silvius – Silvia, Antonius – Antonia, Marius – Maria,
Valerius – Valeria, Annius – Annia, Caecillius – Caecillia, Octavius – Octavia, Junius – Junia,
Tullius – Tullia, Valentinus – Valentina, Livius – Livia, Horatius – Horatia

Cognomen – male only:

Faustus (lucky), Felix (happy), Corvus (raven), Maximus (the greatest), Leo (lion),
Marinus (of the sea), Victor (winner, conqueror)

Additional Latin *cognomen* nicknames for girls:

Laeta (joyful), Beata (blessed), Pia (God-loving), Marina (of the sea), Sylvana (of the woods),
Stella (star), Luna (moon), Aurora (sunrise), Clara (bright), Rosa (a rose), Regina (queen),
Magna (great), Alba (white, bright), Florentina (floral, blooming), Prima (firstborn)

LESSON II

You are certainly familiar with the constellations of the Zodiac.

Let's list their Latin names and see if they are masculine, feminine, or neuter; singular or plural:

Aries – the ram – m.

Gemini – the twins – m. plural; singular: *geminus* – a male twin

Pisces – the fish – m. plural; singular *piscis*

Sagittarius – the archer – m.

Aquarius – the water carrier – m.

Scorpio – the scorpion – m.

Taurus – the bull – m.

Cancer – the crab – m.

Virgo – the girl – f.

Capricornus – the goat – m.

Leo – the lion – m.

Libra – the scales – f.

Proverbia et Dicta

1. *Finis coronat opus.* – The end crowns the work.
2. *Ora et labora.* – Pray and work.
(motto of the Benedictine monks order)
3. *Ego sum Dominus Deus tuus...*
I am Lord your God... (from the 10 Commandments
in the Old Testament of the Bible – Exodus 20:2)

MUA-HA-HA-HA!
SERPENS MAGNUS, MALUS,
TERRIBILIS, ET AUREUS SUM.
AMO SERPERE!

'Roman family' by Emilio Vasarri

WHILE THE KIDS ARE PLAYING,
LET'S GO OVER PLURAL
ENDINGS OF LATIN NOUNS!

I CAN'T WAIT!

GRAMMAR: Latin Verbs and Conjugations

> VOLO!
> AMO VOLARE!

English verbs have only two forms in the present tense:

work – works, write – writes, do – does

Latin verbs have several forms in the present tense. For example:

amare – to love

SINGULAR   PLURAL

I love – *amo*   we love – *amamus*

you love – *amas*   you (more than 1 person) love – *amatis*

he/she/it loves – *amat*   they love – *amant*

amare – to love

habere – to have

videre – to see – video

tenere – to hold – tenacious

scire – to know – science

nescire – to not know

magnus – big – magnificent

parvus – small

Latin verbs can be organized into groups we call 'conjugations.' Inside each group, verbs change forms – or conjugate – in the same way. *Amare* – 'love' belongs to the **1st Conjugation** group. All the verbs in this group have the same present tense endings:

SINGULAR   *- o - as - at*
PLURAL   *- amus - atis - ant*

So if you remember the six forms for **amare**, you will also know the forms of words like

spectare – to look   *specto – spectas – spectat*
                            spectamus – spectatis – spectant

volare – to fly   *volo – volas – volat*
                            volamus – volatis – volant

Spectamus. – We are watching. *Aquila volat*. – An eagle flies.

novus – new – novelty, novel

antiquus – old, ancient

bonus – good

malus – bad – malfunction, malificent

verus – true

falsus – false

aureus – golden

argenteus – silver (adjective)

tuus – your

meus – my

insula f. – island – insulation

The verb *videre* – 'to see' belongs to the **2nd Conjugation** group. The present tense endings for this group are:

SINGULAR   *- eo - es - et*
PLURAL   *- emus - etis - ent*

I see – *video*   we see – *videmus*

you see – *vides*   you (more than 1 person) see – *videtis*

he/she/it sees – *videt*   they see – *vident*

So if you remember the present tense endings for *videre*,

you also know the forms of words like *habere* – to have, or *tenere* – to hold.

habere   *tenere*

habeo – habes – habet   *teneo – tenes – tenet*

habemus – habetis – habent   *tenemus – tenetis – tenent*

> DON'T
> YOU JUST LOVE
> LATIN VERBS?

> Dicit quod nihil habet, nihil videt.

> Quid habes?

> Nihil habeo.

> Quid vides?

> Nihil video!

> He says he has nothing, he sees nothing.

> Yep. Scribit.

For the **3rd Conjugation**, the verbal endings in the present tense are:

- *o - is - it*
- *imus - itis - unt*

RANA

> Scribit! Scribit! Scribit!

Example: *scribere* – to write
scribo – scribis – scribit
scribimus – scribitis – scribunt
Whenever I introduce a new verb
I will indicate its conjugation
group like this: (1), (2), (3).

Moving on! There are two ways
to say 'I have' in Latin –
using *est* – is, or *habere* – have.

To say 'I have a pen' Romans would say, 'Is to me a pen.'
Est mihi stylus.
Estne tibi stylus? – Do you have a pen? 'Is to you a pen?'
Estne tibi liber? Est mihi liber.

You can use the same phrase to ask about a person's name.
Quod nomen est tibi? Mihi nomen est Flavia.
quod – what, which

Using *habere*, you can ask:
The answer will be: *Ita, habeo stylum.*
Now, why *stylum* and not *stylus?*?

> Habes stylum?

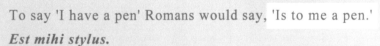

Have you heard the expression
"Speak of the devil..."? You use it
when you are talking about someone,
and, suddenly, that person appears.
Guess what: Ancient Romans had
a similar expression, only rather than
the devil they had a wolf!
lupus – wolf
So, instead of saying
"Speak of the devil,"
Romans said, *Lupus in fabula!* –
'The wolf in a story!' or
'Speak of the wolf and it will come!'

> Wolf! Run everyone!

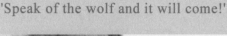

GRAMMAR: Latin Nouns – Accusative Case Singular

When Latin nouns change their forms we call this declension.
We decline nouns by changing their endings.

In English only pronouns have declension. For example, we say
'He plays' but 'I see him.'
'He' is a 'subject' pronoun, and 'him' is an 'object' pronoun.
Subject – object: she – her, we – us, they – them.
In Latin every noun has an 'object' form, which is called the
Accusative case.

stylus – Nominative case, or the subject form
stylum – Accusative case, or the object form of a noun.

Want to hear a joke
about Latin grammar?
"I was asked to conjugate
a Latin verb, but I prefer
nouns, so I declined."
to CONJUGATE A VERB
= to change forms of a verb
to DECLINE A NOUN
= to change forms of a noun

In everyday speech English
verb 'to decline' means either
'to politely refuse,' or
'to get weaker, to fade away.'
It comes from the Latin
declinare (1) - to bend

Want another joke?
"Latin teachers don't get old.
They decline."

I ACCUSE YOU!

IT'S EASY! I PROMISE!

Accusative case is the same as 'direct object' in English, when
an action of a verb directly involves a noun. Examples: 'I see him... I hold a book.'
Video stylum – I see a pen   •   *Teneo stylum* – I hold a pen   •   *Habeo stylum* – I have a pen
I know what you are thinking – How in the world am I going to remember all those forms?!
Well, just like verbs, nouns are organized in groups – in declensions.
If you know the forms of one noun in each declension group, you know them all!

dominus – dominum   *magister – magistrum*   *discipulus – discipulum*   *amicus – amicum*

Even easier: Neuter nouns always have the same ending in the Nominative and Accusative cases!!!

argentum – argentum   *aurum – aurum*   *templum – templum*   *nomen – nomen*

I (1st Declension) – these are mostly feminine nouns ending in *-a*
In the Accusative case their ending is - *am*

  silva – silvam • *lingua – linguam*
Video terram! Vides pennam?

By the way, the state of Pennsylvania has *silva* – forest – in it!
The colony of Pennsylvania – one of the 13 original American colonies – was founded
by William Penn. 'Pennsylvania' - means Penn's woods/forests!

II (2nd Declension) – masculine and neuter nouns ending in - *us, - er. - r, - ir, - um*
Accusative case ending - *um*

cactus m. – *cactum* • *donum* (gift) n. – *donum*
Teneo donum. Habeo cactum.

III (3rd Declension) – the Accusative case endings are
- *em* for masculine and feminine nouns.
Neuter – the same as in the Nominative case.

rex (king) m. – *regem* • *animal* n. – *animal*
Video regem. Amo animal.

> WHAT? THERE ARE
> 5 DECLENSIONS IN LATIN??
> OH, NO. 3 IS ENOUGH
> FOR NOW!

> CHILL!
> 4TH AND 5TH DECLENSIONS
> ACCUSATIVE ENDINGS
> ARE JUST - UM AND - EM

Many Latin sayings and proverbs use the Accusative case of nouns. I want you to read these Latin
sayings and come up with a story showing how you could use one of these sayings in a
conversation. For example: My dad told me, 'Make sure you use the ending - *am* with the
1st Declension nouns in the Accusative case!' And I said, *Aquilam volare doces, pater!*

Aquilam volare doces. – You are teaching (*doces*) an eagle to fly!
Delphinum / piscem natare doces. – You are teaching a dolphin / a fish how to swim.
Felicitas multos habet amicos. – Prosperity has many friends.
Ficus ficus, ligonem ligonem vocat. – He calls a fig a fig, a spade
a spade (straightforward person).
Gratia gratiam parit. – Kindness produces kindness.
Mens bona regnum possidet. – A good mind possesses a kingdom.

...when you realize you learned more grammar
in one year of Latin than you did in ten years of English.

GRAMMAR: Latin Adjectives – Gender, Number, Declension

Ok, we've talked about Latin verbs and nouns, but what about adjectives? Eeeeeeeeasy!
Latin adjectives are copycats! They copy the endings of nouns!

First of all, they copycat the masculine/feminine/neuter endings of nouns:

aqua frigida – cold water • *terra incognita* – unknown land
rivus parvus – small river • *persona non grata* – unwelcome person

Sh-h-h-h-h! Personae non gratae sumus!

Adjectives also copycat the plural endings of nouns:

Estis discipuli novi? Sumus discipuli novi.

Then, those copycat adjectives copycat the noun endings in the Accusative case:

Video silvam magnam. Habeo stylum novum. Video aquam argenteam.

These adjectives are so predictable! Yawn.

More shocking news: Possessive pronouns like

meus – my, mine • *tuus* – your, yours

are also copycats!! *Vere!* (Really! It's true!)

amicus tuus • *amica tua* • *monstrum tuum magnum*

Some words, like *magister, liber,* or *nomen* don't have
the ending *-us or -um.* The adjective will copy the more common *- us* ending of masculine nouns
in the Nominative case, and will echo the noun endings in the the Accusative case:

magister novus – Video magistrum novum.
liber antiquus – Habeo librum antiquum.
plumbum novum – Habeo plumbum novum.

PLUMBUM

Quid est tuum nomen? – What's your name?
Meum nomen Flavia est, or *Est mihi nomen Flavia.*
Can you tell me your name in Latin?

Plures adorant solem orientem quam occidentem.
More people worship the rising sun than the setting sun.
Cor unum, via una. – One heart, one way.

'Thank you', in Latin, is:
Gratias or *Ago tibi gratias.*
Also: *Ago vobis gratias.*
(thanking more than one person)
'Welcome' is: *Libenter* (gladly)
or *Certe* (certainly), or
Nihil est (it's nothing).

Gratia in Latin means 'kindness,
favor, gratitude.' Many English
words come from this root:
grateful, ungrateful, gratitude,
ingratiate (flatter and do favors),
gratis (for free),
gratuity (a tip for a service),
grace, graceful, gracious.

'Please' in Latin is *quaeso* –
'I ask, I beg'

HOMEWORK
Translation

Is your name Julius? • My name is not Julius. My name is Flavius. • My book is good.
The forest is big and bad. Is your new teacher good? • Your book is small. • I have a new book.
I see water. • I see a new friend (male). • I see a new friend (female). • He is holding a big book.
Your new teacher is Mrs.Brown (Domina Brown). • Do you have a good pen?
Are you my new teachers? • We are not your new teachers. • We are new students.
I have a golden pen. • My story is true. • The new stories are good.

> *AQUA PROFUNDA EST QUIETA*
> 'STILL WATER RUNS DEEP'

Reading 1 *Familia Romana*

Personae (characters): *Marcus (puer), Claudia (puella), Claudius (pater), Valeria (mater)*

Claudius: Marce! Marce! Ubi est stylus meus?

Marcus: Claudia habet stylum tuum.

Claudius: Claudia! Ubi est stylus meus, quaeso?

Claudia : Marcus habet stylum tuum.

Claudius: Quid???? Quis habet stylum meum?

Marcus: Claudia!

Claudia: Non habeo! Is habet!

Claudius: Liberi! Non intellego! Marcus dicit
quod Claudia stylum habet, sed Claudia dicit
quod Marcus stylum habet. Ubi est stylus meus???

Marcus et Claudia: Nescimus!

Claudius: Valeria! Valeria!

Valeria: Quid est?

Claudius: Liberi stylum meum habent, sed dicunt
quod nesciunt ubi stylus est!

Valeria: Di boni! Liberi improbi! Ubi est stylus???

puer – boy, *puella* – girl

Marce – the address form of 'Marcus'
When you address a person whose name
ends in – *us*, the name changes its ending
to - *e. Marcus >> Marce!*

quod – that

ubi – where

is – he

Quid est? – What is it? What's going on?

liberi – children

dicunt – they say

nescimus – we don't know

Di boni! – Good gods!

improbus – behaving badly

'Roman Street Scene' by Ettore Forti

MATER PUELLA AQUA PUER IMPROBUS!

Reading 2 *Schola*

Quis est Iulius? Iulius non vir, sed puer est. Iulius discipulus bonus est.

Magistra Flavia videt discipulum et dicet: "Salve! Quid est nomen tibi?"

Iulius videt magistram et respondet: "Et tu salve, Magistra! Nomen meum Iulius est."

Magistra Flavia interrogat: "Esne meus discipulus novus?"

Iulius respondet: "Vero. Tuus discipulus novus sum."

"Bene est. Estne Britannia patria tua?"

Iulius respondet: "Minime. Patria mea non Britannia est. Americanus sum."

Iulius non Anglicus est. Iulius in America Foederata habitat, in urbe Silva Oceanica.

America non est insula. America est terra magna. Britannia insula est.

Magistra Flavia quoque Americana est. Habitat in Urbe Novum Eboracum.

Novum Eboracum urbs magna est. Urbs Silva Oceanica parva est.

Magistra Flavia interrogat: "Habes librum Latinum et tabulam?"

Iulius respondet: "Habeo."

"Habes stylum?"

"Habeo stylum argenteum."

Flavia tenet cartam.

Iulius interrogat: "Quid est?"

Flavia respondet:

"Hic est Europa. Hic est Oceanus Atlanticus."

interrogare (1) – to ask – interrogate

respondere (2) – respond

bene est – great – benefit, beneficiary

patria – homeland – patriotism

habitare (1) – to live – habitat

America Foederata – United States

Urbs Novum Eboracum – New York City

'Recital' by Gugliemo Zocchi

ANCIENT ROMANS COULDN'T GET ENOUGH OF LATIN GRAMMAR.

LESSON III

GRAMMAR: Latin Pronouns

'How are you?' in Latin is:
Quid agis? – 'What do you do?'
'What are you up to?'
Response: *Bene* – Doing well
  Male – Not good
Quantum tempus! –
Long time no see!
Bona Fortuna! – Good luck!

Time to learn the Latin personal pronouns!

I – *ego*   you – *tu*   he – *is*   she – *ea*   it – *id*

we – *nos*   you (more than one person) – *vos*

they (male) – *ei*   they (female) – *eae*   they (neuter, things) – *ea*

Everything looks normal here except the three 'theys' – masculine, feminine and neuter!

Well, at least it's easy to remember them because they have

the same endings as plural nouns (more copycats!) Look:

mascuine plural nouns: ending - *i* – *libri, discipuli* >> *ei* – they (masculine plural)

feminine plural nouns: ending - *ae* – *silvae, magistrae* >> *eae* – they (feminine plural)

neuter plural nouns: ending - *a* – *templa, nomina* >> *ea* – they (neuter plural)

Ego interrogo, tu respondes. – I ask, you respond.

Nos interrogamus, vos respondetis. – We ask, you (plural) answer.

Tu interrogas, ei respondent. – You ask, they (masculine) respond.

Lego librum. Is bonus est. – I am reading a book. It (he) is good.

Ea est nova magistra. – She is a new teacher.

Nos sumus discipuli. – We are students.

CASEUS
MEUS EST.

agere (3) – to act – action, active

legere (3) – to read – lecture

caseus m. – cheese

And here are possessive pronouns:

meus – my, mine   *tuus* – your, yours   *suus* – his, their   *noster* – our   *vester* – your (plural)

They behave pretty much like adjectives, echoing the endings of nouns.

'The Chariot Race' by Alexander von Wagner

CIRCUS

SPECTATORES

EQUI

'A Street Scene' by John William Godward

Labels on image:
- PATER MEUS
- CASA NOSTRA
- AMICI MEI
- VALERIA, AMICA MEA
- CLAUDIA, FILIA SUA
- FLOS SUUS
- VIA NOSTRA
- VALENTINA SUM.
- FLORES MEI
- COLUMBAE
- URBS NOSTRA

GRAMMAR: Nouns – Genitive Case Singular

How do you say in Latin: 'a teacher's book' or 'a page of a book'? In English we use either possessive forms of nouns like 'teacher's' or phrases with the preposition 'of.' In Latin we use a special form of nouns called the **Genitive case** – also known as the Possessive case.

For example, the Genitive case of *magister* is *magistri* – *liber magistri* = teacher's book
the Genitive case of *puella* is *puellae* – *pater puellae* = girl's father
Ratio est radius divini luminis. – Reason is a ray of divine light (Gen. case of ***divinum lumen***)

Some Latin nouns have one stem in the Nominative case, and a different stem in all other cases. For example ***ratio – rationis.*** So if you know the Genitive case of a noun, you can easily figure out all its forms! That's why Latin dictionaries give you two forms for each noun: Nominative case and Genitive case, plus its gender and declension for example: ***ratio – rationis*** f. (3)

Declension	Nominative Case ending	Genitive Case ending	
1st	*-a*	*- ae*	*terra – terrae f.*
2nd	*-us, -r, -er, -ir, - um*	*- i*	*amicus - amici m.*
3rd	*-x, -s , - is, - e, - n & more*	*- is*	*nomen - nominis n.*
4th	*-us*	*- us*	*senatus - senatus m.*
5th	*-es*	*- ei*	*res - rei f. (things, matters)*

The beautiful Italian countryside! Here is a list of some objects you see in this picture, sorted by their owner. Some of them belong to my friend's family, some to the country of Italy, and others to God. I also indicate noun gender and declensions (1), (2), (3), etc.

	Nominative	Accusative	Belong to (Genitive)
country house	*villa rustica f. (1)*	*villam rusticam*	*familiae amici*
garden	*hortus m. (2)*	*hortum*	*familiae amici*
field	*campus m. (2)*	*campum*	*familiae amici*
woods	*silva f. (1)*	*silvam*	*familiae amici*
grass	*herba f. (1)*	*herbam*	*familiae amici*
tree	*arbor f. (3)*	*arborem*	*familiae amici*
town	*urbs f. (3)*	*urbem*	*Italiae*
mountain	*mons m. (3)*	*montem*	*Italiae*
sky	*caelus m. (2)*	*caelum*	*Dei*
clouds	*nubes f. (3)*	*nubes*	*Dei*
sun	*sol m. (3)*	*solem*	*Dei*

Quid?? Caelus meus est!

We are going to make Latin sentences with the above words – three sentences for each word. E.g.:

1. This is the sky (use the Nominative case.) Please use the words

   hic – this (masculine)   *haec* – this (feminine)   *hoc* – this (neuter)

2. I see the sky (use the Accusative case).

3. The sky is God's (the Genitive case).

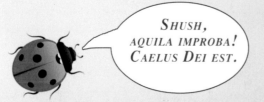

Shush, aquila improba! Caelus Dei est.

Do you know this abbreviation:

e.g. – exempli gratia

This is how you say 'for example' in Latin.

gratia – thanks to

exempli – Genitive case of *exemplum* n. (2)

Here are a few Latin phrases and sayings that use the Genitive case of nouns. Please come up with an example showing how you could use one of these sayings in a conversation.

historia vitae magistra – history, the teacher of life
vita – vitae f. (1) – life – vital, vitality
ignorantia juris non excusat – ignorance of law is no excuse
jus – juris n. (3) – law
initium sapientiae timor Domini - the beginning of wisdom
is the fear of the Lord (from Psalm 111)
sapientia – sapientiae f. (1) – wisdom
Veritatis simplex oratio est. – The language (oratio) of truth is simple.
veritas – veritatis f. (3)
opus Dei – work of God
fortunae filius – a son of Fortune (a lucky person)
lapsus linguae – a slip of a tongue
Felix dies natalis! – Happy Birthday! (*natalis – natalis* m. (3)– birthday)

The name of semiprecious stone, *lapis lazuli*, comes from the Latin words *lapis – lapidis* m. – stone, and the Genitive case of *lazulum – lazuli* n. (2) – sky, blue color

'Friends' by Cesare Mariani

I have a map of the United States, and of New York City where I live.
Habeo cartam Amercae Foederatae et cartam Urbis Novi Eboraci.
What maps do you have? A map of America, of Europe, of the world? Tell me in Latin!
urbs mea f. (3) – my city/town
America f. (1) – America
America Foederata – United States
Europa f. (1) – Europe
mundus – mundi m. (2) – world – mundane

Romans loved murals! They didn't hang pictures on the walls of their houses. Instead, they hired artists to paint flowers, gods, and scenes from history directly on the walls – inside and outside!
The word 'mural' comes from
murus – muri m. (2) – wall

DOMUS

AVIS

PUELLA

CANIS

HOMEWORK

Translation

Albae gallinae filius – the son of a white hen = a lucky person. Ancient Romans used this expression when talking of men who were successful in whatever they undertook.

The wolf is the king of the forest. • My friend is the queen of a big land. • glory (gloria) of Europe glory of the king • map of a big land • king of the world • king's book • queen's book silver water of the forest • map of an island • treasure (*thesaurus* m. (2)) of a pirate (*pirata* m. (1))

Proverbia et Dicta

CARTA INSULAE

1. *Memento mori.* – Remember death (remember that you are mortal.)
2. *Honora patrem tuum et matrem tuam.* – Honor your father and your mother. (From the 10 Commandments, the Old Testament of the Bible, Exodus 20:12)
3. *Sic transit gloria mundi.* – So leaves the glory of this world (the words said during the coronation of a new Pope.)

THESAURUS PIRATAE

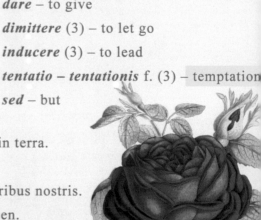

Pater Noster – Our Father – are the first words of the Lord's Prayer. There are a few other possessive pronouns in the Lord's Prayer:

nomen tuum – your name

regnum tuum – your kingdom

voluntas tua – your will

panem nostrum – our bread – Accusative case (Nominative: *panis noster*)

debita nostra – our debts/sins – plural Accusative case (Nominative singular: *debitum nostrum*)

oremus – let's pray

qui – who

caelus – caeli m. (2) – sky, heaven

sanctificetur – be sanctified, be holy

adveniat – may come

fiat – may be done

sicut – like, similar to

dare – to give

dimittere (3) – to let go

inducere (3) – to lead

tentatio – tentationis f. (3) – temptation

sed – but

Reading 1
The Lord's Prayer in Latin

Oremus.

In nomine Patris, et Filii, et Spiritus Sancti. Amen.

Pater noster, qui es in caelis, sanctificetur nomen tuum.

Adveniat regnum tuum. Fiat voluntas tua, sicut in caelo, et in terra.

Panem nostrum quotidianum da nobis hodie,

et dimitte nobis debita nostra sicut et nos dimittimus debitoribus nostris.

Et ne nos inducas in tentationem, sed libera nos a malo. Amen.

Reading 2 *Familia Romana*

Personae: Marcus (puer), Claudia (puella), Valeria (mater), Ferox (canis)

Claudia: Ferox, cape pilam!

Ferox: Baubau!

Claudia: Canis bonus! Cape pilam!

Ferox: Baubau!

Marcus: Claudia, Ferox canis meus est.

Claudia: Immo, Marce, Ferox canis meus est!

Marcus: Et haec pilla mea est quoque.

Claudia: Immo, mea pilla est, et tu puer improbus es!

[Marcus capit pillam.]

Claudia plorat: Siste! Siste! Uh-uhu! Mamma! Mamma!

Valeria: Quid est? Cur puella mea plorat? Cur flos parvus meus plorat? Marce! Cur sororcula tua plorat?

Claudia: Marcus dicit quod Ferox canis Marci est, non canis meus, et pila mea non mea sed Marci est! Marcus pilam meam habet!

Valeria: Marce! Haec pila sororis tuae Claudiae est!

Marcus: Certe. Pila sororis meae est, sed Ferox meus est!

Claudia: Meus! Canicula mea!

Valeria: Liberi! Tacite! Et audite me! Ferox canis patris vestri est! Pater vester canem suum amat.

Ferox: Baubau!

Valeria: Quis canis bonus est? Ferox canis bonus est!

Pila mea est – I've won = I have the ball (a Roman proverb)

immo – no, no way

cape! – catch!

capere (3) – to capture, to catch

pila – pilae f. – ball

Siste! – Stop it! from *sistere* to stop

cur – why

plorat – cries

sororcula – little sister

canicula – doggie, little dog

Tacite! – be silent

Audite! – listen

Romans often used suffix
- culus - cula - culum - cule
to say 'small, tiny'
*sororcul*a – little sister
animalcule – tiny animal
You may notice this suffix in many English words of Latin origin:
molecule – from Latin *moles* – mass
minuscule – from Latin *minuscula* – even smaller
particular – from Latin *particula* – small part
spatula – from Latin *spatha* – broadsword

Have you seen a sign saying 'Beware of the dog'? Guess what: They had those signs in *Roma Antiqua*! Here is proof: *Cave canem* on a mosaic floor in Pompeii in Italy.

cavere (2) – to beware, to avoid

canis – canis m./f. (3) – canine

Pompeii was destroyed during the eruption of Mount Vesuvius volcano in AD 79.

Speaking of which... volcano << *Vulcan* was the Roman god of fire (same as Greek Hephaestus.)

CAVE CANEM

LATIN LEGAL TERMS

Since the days of the Roman empire, lawyers have used a lot of Latin legal (related to law) terms and expressions. In English even the word 'legal' comes from the Latin word *lex – legis* f. (3). Some legal terms are borrowed from Latin without any change, and others are a mix of English and Latin.

jurisprudence – study of law, from *prudentia juris* – knowledge, skill in law, *jus – juris* n. (3)

justuce – from *justitia* f. (1) – justice; jury – from *jurare* (1) – to take an oath, to call to witness

judge, judicial – from *jus* – law + *dicere* – to say; prejudice = pre-judge

alibi – being somewhere else, not on the scene of crime, from Latin *alibi* – elsewhere

modus operandi – 'way of operating' – the way a criminal commits crimes

bona fide – 'in good faith,' said or done without any criminal intent – *fides – fidei* f. (5) – faith

pro bono – 'for the good' – work done without pay, for the public good

in loco parentis – 'in place of a parent' – a grownup, such as a relative or a teacher, making a decision for a kid if parents are not available

cease and desist – a demand to stop a potentially criminal activity – 'cease' comes from Latin *cessare* – leave off; 'desist' comes from the Latin *sistere* – to stop

postmortem – from Latin *post* – after and *mors – mortis* f. (3) – death – examination of a dead body to establish the cause of death

quid pro quo – 'this for that' – exchanging favors

habeas corpus – 'that you have the body' – a petition demanding that authorities explain why a person is detained (to prevent people from being held in jail without a cause.)

'A Show' by Henryk Siemiradzki

Reading 3 – *Schola*

Cornelia et Iulius discipuli sunt. Cornelia amica Iulii est. Iulius amicus Corneliae est.

Magistra sua, Flavia, amat linguam Latinam et scientiam.

"Salvete discipuli!" Flavia dicit. "Quid agitis?"

"Bene, et tu?" discipuli respondent.

"Bene, Deo gratias," Flavia dicit. "Nunc ad opus! Hic est liber Latinus. Legamus."

Flavia et discipuli legunt fabulam latinam. Fabula longa et bona est.

Magistra interrogat Corneliam: "Estne tibi soror?"

"Est mihi soror," Cornelia dicit. "Ea ist puella parva."

"Amas sororem tuam?"

"Amo," respondet Cornelia.

Magistra interrogat Iulium: "Estne tibi frater?"

"Est mihi frater," Iulius respondet.

"Bonus frater est. Hic liber fratris mei est."

"Magistra, quis est pater tuus?"

Cornelia interrogat.

"Pater meus professor universitatis est,

mathematicam docet," Flavia respondet.

"Amatne pater tuus mathematicam docere?"

discipuli interrogant.

"Amat," Flavia respondet,

"Fortuna est parva, sed fama est magna."

"Discipuli mei, ago vobis gratias.

Valete," ea dicit.

Discipuli respondent:

"Gratias, et vale, Magistra Flavia."

Nunc ad opus! – Now to work!

legamus – let's read

vobis – to you

salvete – hello to more than one person

valete – good bye to more than one person

longus – long

universitas – universitatis f. (3) – university

fortuna f. (1) – money, wealth

fama f. (1) – fame, reputation

'A Festival' by John Reinhard Weguelin

LESSON IV

Let's learn colors! To ask 'What color..?' in Latin, say

Qui color....est?

Qui color hic canis est? Estne albus hic canis?

Hic canis niger est.

Qui color flos est? – What color is the flower?

Hic flos flavus est. – The flower is yellow.

Colors are adjectives, so they will have
the adjective endings.

Puer canem nigrum habet. – A boy has a black dog.

Qui color cubiculum tuum est? – What color is your room?

Cubiculum meum album est. – My room is white.

What about your room? Please answer in Latin!

PREPOSITION *In* + Location

Ok, how do we indicate location in Latin?

We can use preposition *in*, for example:

Quid in campo est? Arbor in campo est.

Ubi est arbor? In campo. Nubes sunt in caelo.

Remember, from the Lord's Prayer:

in caelo et in terra – in heaven and on earth

Colores Latini

albus / alba – white – albino

niger / nigra – black – Niger, Nigeria

ruber / rubra – red – ruby, rubric

roseus / rosea – pink – rose, rosy

flavus / flava – yellow

viridis / viride – green – verdant

caeruleus / caerulea – blue – cerulean

purpureus / purpurea – purple

The Latin word for 'room' is

camera – *camerae* f. (1) – chamber

But if it's your bedroom in your
family's house, use the word

cubiculum – *cubicula* n. (2) – cubicle

from *cubare* – to lie down.

Upstairs bedrooms in a Roman
city house (*domus*) or country *villa*
were called *cubicula*.

Notice another familiar word in the
sentence:

Cubiculum meum album est.

The Engish word 'album' comes from
the Latin adjective

albus – white, blank; *album*
is a neuter singular form of *albus*

The preposition *in* is used with the **Ablative case** of nouns.

We already know:

Nominative case – *magister*

Genitive case – *liber magistri*

Accusative case – *video magistrum*

Now let's learn about
the Ablative case. It's easy!

DON'T PANIC.
MAGISTRA SAID
IT'S EASY.

ABL...WH- WH- WHAT?

GRAMMAR: Nouns – Ablative Case Singular

Here is a chart of the noun endings for four cases – Nominative, Genitive, Dative and Ablative.

Declension	Nominative	Genitive	Accusative m.,f.	Ablative
1st	-a	- ae	- am	- a
2nd	-us, -r, -er, -ir, - um	- i	- um	- o
3rd	-x, -s , - is, - e, - n & more	- is	- em	- e, - i
4th	-us	- us	- um	- u
5th	-es	- ei	-em	- e

Notice that in the Accusative Case you see endings only for masculine and feminine nouns, because for neuter nouns Nominative = Accusative.

Examples of using the Ablative case to indicate location – notice gender and declension:

campus m. (2) – *in campo* – in the field

silva f. (1) – *in silva* – in the forest

urbs f. (3) – *in urbe* – in the city

spiritus m. (4) – *in spiritu* – in spirit

manus f. (4) – *in manu* – in hand

futurum n. (2) – *in futuro* – in the future

memoria f. (1) – *in memoriam* – in memory of

e.g. *In memoriam Aemiliae* – in memory of Aemilia

IN FLORE DORMIO

Please answer in Latin:

Ubi es nunc? Where are you now?

In casa? In schola?

Ubi magister tuus laborat?

In casa? In schola? In campo?

Ubi habitas? In Europa? In America?

Ubi dormis? In casa? In campo?

In silva?

Latin sayings using the preposition *in* + Ablative case.

Please come up with an example showing how you could use one of these sayings in a conversation.

For example: I asked my dad, 'Where is my Halloween candy?'

He rolled his eyes, 'It's all over the house!... In mari aquam quaeris!'

Mens sana in corpore sano. – A healthy mind in a healthy body.

In bono veritas – Truth is in the good.

In nocte consilium. – At night counsel/advice ("Sleep on it.")

In aqua scribis. – You are writing on water (you are wasting your time).

In arena aedificas. – You are building on sand.

In mari aquam quaerit. – In the sea he is looking for water.

Silentium est aureum. – Silence is gold (golden).

corpus – corporis n. (3) – body

bonum – boni n. (2) – good

nox – noctis f. (3) – night

arena f. (1) – sand

mare – maris n. (3) – sea

DRACO

BACULUM MAGICUM HABEO!

By the Fountain' by Henryk Siemiradzki

As always, there are a few crazy, ancient, irregular words to rain on our parade!

'At home' is *domi* – no preposition *in*. 'In the countryside' is *ruri* – no *in*.

Est Dominus Brown domi? – Is Mr.Brown at home?

Habito ruri. – I live in the country.

Ancient Romans called the Italian island of Capri the 'Goat Island' – from *caper – capri* m. (2) – goat

Look at the picture above and answer the questions:

Ubi sunt nubes? (in the sky) **Ubi est arbor?** (in the field)

Ubi sunt puer et puella? (in the garden *hortus – horti* m. (3))

Ubi puer habitat? (in the country) **Ubi sunt capri?** (on the road *via* f. (1))

Ubi est rivus? (in the forest) **Ubi est pater puellae?** (in town)

Ubi est mater pueri? (at home) **Ubi sunt pisces?** (in the water)

OH THE TIMES! OH THE MORALS!

Cicero and Catilina by Cesare Maccari

O TEMPORA! O MORES!

LUCIUS SERGIUS CATILINA IN SENATU AUDIT.

MARCUS TULLIUS CICERO IN SENATU DICIT.

UBI EST GAIUS JULIUS CAESAR? DOMI DORMIT!

GRAMMAR: Nouns – Dative Case Singular

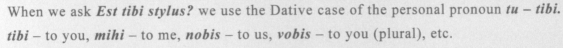

CENA

Let's learn one more case of Latin nouns – the **Dative case.**

Dative case is used whenever something is being transferred or given to someone.

Ago tibi gratias – I thank you, or I give thanks to you

Gloria tibi, Domine – Glory be to you, Lord

When we ask *Est tibi stylus?* we use the Dative case of the personal pronoun *tu – tibi.*

tibi – to you, *mihi* – to me, *nobis* – to us, *vobis* – to you (plural), etc.

You already know these forms!

You can use Dative case when you talk about giving something to someone:

Da mihi – Give me   *Da nobis* – Give us

In the Lord's Prayer, *Panem nostrum quotidianum da nobis hodie* – our daily bread give us today

da mihi pecuniam – give me money (*pecunia – pecuniae* f. (1) - money)

da mihi librum – give me a book

MALUM

Da is the command form of the Latin verb *dare* – to give

Actually the term 'Dative case' comes from *dare.*

Da mihi florem! – Give me a flower.   *Do tibi florem.* – I give you a flower.

Let's make a few sentences. Ask in Latin for a book, a writing tablet, water, a goat (just kidding!)

What are the endings of the nouns in the Dative case?

SANDALIUM

Here is a new chart that includes Dative case singluar!

Declension	Nominative	Genitive	Dative	Accusative m.,f.	Ablative
1st	-a	- ae	- ae	- am	- a
2nd	-us, -r, -er, -ir, - um	- i	- o	- um	- o
3rd	-x, -s , - is, - e, - n + more	- is	- i	- em	- e, - i
4th	-us	- us	- u, -ui	- um	- u
5th	-es	- ei	- ei	- em	- e

epistula dominae – a letter to the lady • *donum puellae* – a gift to a girl

Deo gratias. – Thanks be to God. • *Quid cenae?* – What's for dinner? – *cena* f. (1)

Gratias agamus Domino Deo nostro. – Let us give thanks to the Lord our God.

Flamma fumo est proxima. – Fire is close to the smoke (Where there's smoke, there's fire.)

Forti et fideli nihil difficile. – To a brave and faithful [person] mothing is difficult.

OK, are you ready for another crazy, ancient Latin verb?

velle – to want, wish – voluntary, volunteer

It's just as ancient as *esse* – to be. As long as people have existed, they have wanted this and that!

volo – I want   *vis* – you want   **vult** – he/she wants

volumus – we want   *vultis* – you (more than one person) want   *volunt* – they want

Volo discere. – I want to learn/study. *Volo laborare.* – I want to work. *Volo legere.* – I want to rea

Qui totum vult totum perdit. – He who wants everything loses everything.

Deo volente – God willing, if nothing prevents it...

Deus vult – God wills – the motto of European knights during crusades

Cattus amat pisces, sed non vult tingere plantas. – A cat likes fish, but doesn't want to wet its paws.

Tell me what you want in Latin: *Vis discere aut docere? Vis laborare aut dormire?*

Vis in casa aut in schola esse? Vis in Europa aut America habitare? Vis cantare?

Vis librum scribere? Vis librum legere? Vis multas terras et insulas videre?

MENSA

Believe it or not, to say 'I don't want' in Latin, you use a totally different verb!

nolle = *velle* + *non*! CraZZZZeeeeeeeeee!

nolo – I don't want   *non vis* – you don't want   *non vult* – he/she doesn't want

nolumus – we don't want   *non vultis* – you (plural) don't want   *nolunt* – they don't want

That's a lot. You need a break. Tell me (in Latin) what you don't want to do right now:

'I don't want to work / to learn / to speak / to read / to write!' Volo dormire!

There is even a Latin expression that uses both *velle* and *nolle*:

Volens nolens – 'whether you want it or not.'

DID SOMEBODY JUST SAY 'WOLF'?

Proverbia et Dicta

1. *Lupus non timet canem latrantem.* – A wolf is not afraid of a barking dog.

2. *Mala herba cito crescit.* – Bad grass grows fast (evil spreads fast.)

3. *Gloria in excelsis Deo et in terra pax.* – Glory to God in the highest and on earth peace.

Quaenam est tempestas hodie? – What is the weather today?

Frigidum aut calidum? Pluit aut ningit? Tell me in Latin!

SELLA

 caelum serenum
sol lucet

 pluit

 tempestas

calidum

tepidum

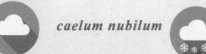 *caelum nubilum*   *ningit*   *ventosum*

frigidum

GRAMMAR: Accusative Case Plural

Video magistrum. With a direct object of an action – *magistrum* – we use the Accusative case.
What if you see a group of teachers? We'll use the Accusative case plural: *Video magistros.*
Here is a chart for the Accusative case plural endings by declension:

Declension	Nominative	Nominative Plural	Accusative m.,f.	Accusative Plural
1st	-a	- ae	- am	- as
2nd	-us, -r, -er, -ir, - um	- i, - a	- um	- os (m., f.) - a (n.)
3rd	-x, -s , - is, - e, - n + more	- es, -a	- em	- es, -a (same as Nom.pl.)
4th	-us	- us, - ua	- um	- us, - ua (same as Nom.pl.)
5th	-es	- es	- em	- es (same as Nom.pl.)

Veros amicos reparare dificile est. – It is difficult to replace true friends.
margaritas ante porcos – [throwing] pearls before swine (from the Gospel of Matthew 7:6)
Quid vides in via? What do you see in the street of Pompeii? Use the Accusative case plural.
arbor f. (3) – a tree, *sculptura* f. (1) – a sculpture, *equus* m. (2) – a horse, *femina* f. (1) – a woman
flos m. (3) – flower, *liberi* (plural) – children, *domus* f. (4) – house, *templum* n. (2) – temple
columna f. (1) – column, *currus* m. (4) – *currus* pl. – chariot, *porta* f. (1) – gate
Uh-oh. Look at that smoking Vesuvius - the volcano that destroyed the town of Pompeii in AD 79.

LATIN MILITARY TERMS

Guess where else you find a lot of Latin terms?
In the military!

military << *milis – militis* m. (3) – soldier

army, armor << *arma* n. pl. (2) – arms

navy, naval << *navis* f. (3) – ship

fort, fortification << *fortis* – strong

camp, campaign << *campus* m. (2) – field

submarine << *sub* – under, *mare* n. (3) – sea

insignia (badges, stars and other marks

indicating military rank) << *insigne* n. (3)– emblem, badge

ballistic << *ballista* f. (1) – a military machine for throwing stones

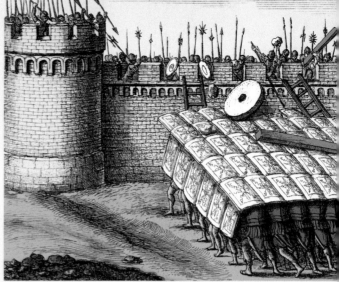

Roman soldiers in a **testudo** (tortoise) formation that
allowed them to approach the enemy unharmed

ballista

HOMEWORK

Reading 1 *Familia Romana*
Personae: Marcus (puer), Claudia (puella), Valeria (mater)

Claudia: Mamma, da mihi tabulam et stylum. Discere et
scribere volo! Doce me litteras.

Valeria: Puella mea bona! Stella mea parva! Flos meus pulcher es! Marce, audi!
Soror tua parva discere vult! Et tu? Discere non vis, scribere non vis, et legere non vis! Cur?

Marcus: Quia ludere volo!

Valeria: Magister tuus dicit quod numeros discere et computare non vis!

Marcus: Scio computare.

Valeria: Quot sunt uno et duo?

Marcus: Tres.

Valeria: Quot sunt uno et tres?

Marcus: Quattuor.

Valeria: Quot sunt duo et tres?

Marcus: Quinque.

Valeria: Bene computas! Puer meus carus, ingeniosus, et prudens es!

Magister malus prave dicit! Amo liberos meos!

stella f. – star

carus – dear

prudens – wise

ingeniosus – talented

prave – incorrectly, wrongly

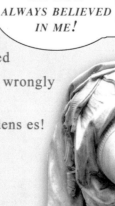

MY MOM
ALWAYS BELIEVED
IN ME!

Reading 2 – *Schola*

Ubi sunt Cornelia et Iulius? Domi? Domi non sunt. Ubi sunt? Hi discipuli sunt in schola.

Nolunt in casa esse! Volunt in schola discere. Scribunt et legunt. Magistra quoque est in schola.

Magistra vult docere. Magistra interrogat: "Ubi vultis habitare – in urbe aut ruri?"

"In urbe," dicit Iulius.

hi – these (plural)

"Ruri" dicit Cornelia, "quod amo silvas et rivos."

"Quid est in silvis?" interrogat Iulius.

"Multae arbores pulchrae, herba, et flores illic sunt. Et in rivis sunt pisces aurei."

"Suntne animalia illic?"

"Aves in silvis habitant."

"Suntne animalia mala illic quoque?" Iulius interrogat.

"Certe, sunt lupi in silvis," Cornelia respondet.

"Nolo ruri habitare," Iulius dicit.

WHO SAID 'WOLF'?

IS THAT LATIN? SO ANNOYING.

THAT'S WHAT HORSES SPOKE IN ANCIENT ROME.

QUIS DIXIT 'LUPUS'? SCISNE DE LUPO IN FABULA?

❦ LESSON V ❦

GRAMMAR: Nouns – Genitive Case Plural

I WARNED YOU.

We use the Genitive case to indicate that something belongs to someone.

liber discipuli – student's book

What if there is a group of students, and it's their book? We'll need the Genitive case plural of the word 'students' – *discipulorum – liber discipulorum.*

Most Latin nouns have endings - *rum* in Genitive case plural. Some have endings - *um* and - *ium*.

Declension	Nominative	Genitive Singular	Genitive Plural
1st	*-a*	*- ae*	*- arum*
2nd	*-us, -r, -er, -ir, - um*	*- i*	*- orum*
3rd	*-x, -s , - is, - e, - n + more*	*- is*	*- um, - ium*
4th	*-us*	*- us*	*- uum*
5th	*-es*	*- ei*	*-erum*

Diana est dea silvarum. – Diana is the goddess of the forests. • *donum amicorum* – friends' gift
rex marium – king of the seas • *ira deorum* – wrath of the gods
multorum annorum opus – the work of many years • *Gravis ira regum semper.* – Always heavy is the anger of kings. • *Hypocritae progenies viperarum.* – Hypocrites are the offspring of vipers.
Mater artium necessitas. – Necessity is the mother of the arts (inventions.)

'A Family' by Gugliemo Zocchi

BENE!

FLOS — FLORUM
CAMPUS — CAMPORUM
ARBOR — ARBORUM
URBS — URBIUM

IN ANCIENT ROME EVEN BABIES KNEW GENITIVE CASE PLURAL.

Some expressions from the Bible that use the plural Genitive case of nouns are:

Sanctum Sanctorum – the Holy of Holies (or *Sancta Sanctorum* – the Holies of the Holies)

in saecula saeculorum – unto the ages of ages (also translated as 'forever and ever')

Would you like to be a King – *Rex*, or a Queen – *Regina*? Let's crown you!

What would your royal title be? Are you the King / Queen

of flowers (*florum*)? of trees? (*arborum*) of birds? (*avum*) of animals? (*animalium*)

of seas? (*marium*), of roads (*viarum*), of unknown lands (*terrarum incognitarum*) ...

Say it in Latin: *Sum Rex / Regina* + Genitive case plural...

PREPOSITION *De*

How do we say in Latin 'about'?

We use the preposition *de* + Ablative case.

fabula de silva magica

fabula de vita in Europa

Non hoc de nihilo est. – This is not about nothing (There is truth in this story.)

QUID CENAE?

NOLO!

VIS PANEM?

VOLO CANDY ET PIZZA!

VIS PISCEM?

GRAMMAR: Nouns – Ablative and Dative Cases Plural

What if you want to say 'a story about animals'? 'Animals' is plural. We need the Ablative case plural.

Great News! For most Latin nouns Ablative and Dative cases plural have the same forms!!!!

So we are learning plural forms for two cases! Woohoo!

Declension	Nominative	Dative Singular	Ablative Singular	Ablative / Dative Plural
1st	*-a*	*- ae*	*- a*	*- is*
2nd	*-us, -r, -er, -ir, - um*	*- o*	*- o*	*- is*
3rd	*-x, -s , - is, - e*	*- i*	*- e, - i*	*- ibus*
4th	*-us*	*- u, - ui*	*- u*	*- ibus*
5th	*-es*	*- ei*	*- e*	*- ebus*

fabula de regibus magnis, rivis argenteis, de silvis magicis, de arboribus albis

Falsus in uno, falsus in omnibus. – False in one thing, false in everything.

Omnibus is Ablative case plural of *omnis* – all, everything. • *Cede nullis.* – Yield to no one.

Please answer in Latin:

Amas fabulas de animalibus aut de hominibus? Amas fabulas longas aut breves?

Here are a few Latin sayings. Please come up with a story showing how you could use one of these sayings in a conversation. For example: I asked my dad, 'Where is my coffee cup?' He said, 'Where you left it – on your desk! You are so absent-minded, always *in nubibus*!'

Est modus in rebus. – There is a system (method) in everything.

Omnia bona bonis. – All things are good to good men.

in nubibus – in the clouds (dreaming about something)

in omnia paratus – ready for anything / everything

omnia omnibus – everything for everyone

in pleno – in full – plenty   *in toto* – entirely – total

in silvam ligna ferre – to carry the wood to the forest (to do useless work)

In te, Domine, speravi. – In you, Lord, have I put my trust.

Who else uses Latin all the time? Scientists!

The chemical elements in the Periodic table all have Latin names!

F – ***ferrum*** is iron

Ag – ***argentum*** is silver

Au – ***aurum*** is gold

Cu – ***cuprum*** is copper ('Cyprus' comes from the same root: That's where Europeans mined for copper during the Bronze Age!)

Pb – ***plumbum*** is lead (that's where the word 'plumber' comes from!)

The classification of plant and animal species uses two-part Latin names.

The first part is the **genus** – the family of animals or plants (fox, wolf, rose), the second name describes only one particular species.

grey wolf is ***Canis*** (dog family) ***lupus*** (grey wolf)

red wolf is ***Canis*** (dog family) ***rufus*** (red)

dog is ***Canis*** (dog family) ***familiaris*** (domesticated, lives with human families)

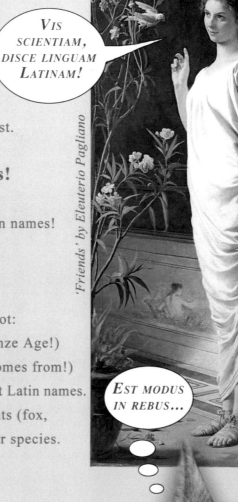

'Friends' by Eleuterio Pagliano

CANIS LUPUS >>
<< CANIS FAMILIARIS

HOMEWORK

Translation:

I want to walk in the forests. • He wants to walk in the fields. • He loves the long road. • She is a queen of white flowers. • Lion (leo) is the king of animals. • I love the story about white birds. She loves the story about friends of the unicorn (*unicorn – unicornis* m. (3)) • I am on an island. I am in the house. • The school is in the forest. • The girls are walking to the school. The girl is carrying a writing tablet to the school. • You don't like islands. • The girls' school...

Proverbia et Dicta

1. *sapienti sat* – a word is enough to the wise – or, in full, 'dictum sapienti sat est' – what was said is enough for the wise – *sapiens* – wise, capable of thinking, as in *homo sapiens*
2. *de gustibus non est disputandum* – 'of tastes there is nothing to be disputed' ("In matters of taste, there can be no disputes")
3. *Fiat Lux.* – Let there be light. – Old Testament of the Bible, Genesis 1:3
'Fiat' is also an Italian car brand founded in 1899. FIAT is an abbreviation of Fabbrica Italiana Automobili Torino (Italian automobile factory of Turin) and the Latin word *fiat* – 'let it be done.'

First Fiat car – Fiat 3½ HP, 1899

Reading 1 – 'Glory Be'

Gloria Patri, et Filio, et Spiritui Sancto. Sicut erat in principio, et nunc, et semper,
et in saecula saeculorum. Amen. Glory be to the Father and to the Son and to the Holy Spirit.
As it was in the beginning, is now, and ever shall be, world without end. Amen.
These are words from Latin prayers and the Catholic Latin mass. In this sentence
Patri, Filio et Spiritui Sancto are the Dative case forms of *Pater, Filius, et Spiritus Sanctus.*

sicut – as, so
erat – was
in principio – in the beginning
semper – always

ECCLESIA

IESUS CHRISTUS

Byzantine mosaic in Chora Church,
Constantinople (Istanbul)

Reading 2 – *Familia Romana*

Personae: Marcus (puer), Valeria (mater), Claudius (pater)

Claudius: Marce! Est mihi epistula magistri tui. Audi. In epistula scribit:

'Salve, Domine. Filius tuus, Marcus Claudius Felix, in schola dormit aut ludit, non audit, non discit. Industrius non est. Prudens non est. Dicsipulus bonus non est. Piger est. Vale. P.S. Scientiam astronomicam discere non vult.'

Valeria: Non credo magistris. Id verum non est! Ille magister morosus est!

Claudius: Magister scribit quod Marcus scientiam astronomicam discere non vult.

Valeria: Marcus scientiam astronomicam amat. Omnes stellas in caelis scit!

Claudius: Specta, Marce! Quid est illa lux clara in caelo – stella aut luna?

Marcus: Luna.

Claudius: Et illa? Stella aut luna?

Marcus: Stella.

Claudius: Scit astronomiam filius meus! Numquam credite magistris!

> *MAGISTER MEUS BENIGNUS, NON MOROSUS EST!*

epistula – epistulae f. (1) – letter

ludere (3) – to play • *piger* – lazy

P.S. – post scriptum = something added at the end of a letter or a book

morosus – difficult to deal with – morose

quod – that • *clarus* – bright

numquam – never

credere – to believe – credible, credentials

credite! – believe! (plural, command)

Reading 3 – *Schola*

Ubi nunc magistra et discipuli sunt? In schola? Non in schola sunt. Dies faustus! Ambulant in silva alta et magna. Cornelia et Iulius laeti sunt. Cornelia cantat "La-la-la!" Cornelia et Iulius vident arborem. In arbore avis nigra sedet. "Tweet-tweet!" avis cantat.

"Intellego linguam avum!" Cornelia dicit.

"Quid? Non credo!" Iulius exclamat.

"Vere," Cornelia dicit. "Intellego linguas avum, et piscium, et omnium animalium."

"Scis quod illa avis dicit?" Iulius interrogat.

"Scio. Avis edere vult," Cornelia respondet.

Iulius et Cornelia rident.

"Homo qui ridet laetus est," dicit Magistra Flavia. Cornelia et Iulius cantant de silvis, et rivis, et floribus.

dies faustus – a lucky day

ambulare (1) – to walk, to travel ambulance, ambulatory

laetus – happy

avis – avis f. (3) - a bird

cantare (1) – to sing

altus – tall – altitude

edere – to eat

ridere (2) – to laugh – ridicule, ridiculous

> *RARA AVIS SUM!*

> *AMICITIA VERA, RARA AVIS IN TERRA.*

LESSON VI

IN LECTO DORMIT

The Latin verb *posse* – 'can, to be able to' is another one of those crazy, ancient verbs!

Just take a look at these forms:

possum – potes – potest

possimus – potestis – possunt

> *POSSUM SUM!*
> *IN ARBORE HABITO.*
> *NOCTURNUM SUM.*
> *FLUFFY SUM.*

Non possimus te videre. – We can't see you.

Possum fabulam narrare. – I can tell a story.

Dum potes, vive. – Live while you can.

a posse ad esse –

from being possible to actually happening

Delegatus non potest delegare. –

A delegate cannot delegate.

> *COMPUTARE*
> *NON POSSUM.*
> *LEGERE NON POSSUM.*
> *DISCIPULUS BONUS*
> *NON SUM.*

Didelphis marsupialis, or the Common Opossum

Quid potes? What can you do at school? Tell me in Latin:

... read a Latin book? write a letter? play? sleep? give gifts? walk in the street? laugh? sing?

PREPOSITION *Ex*

The Latin preposition *ex* means 'from,' 'out of'

E.g.: *ex fenestra* – from a window • *ex silvis* – from the forest • *ex rivis* – from the river

Like many other Latin prepositions *ex* is used with the Ablative case of a noun.

ex pluribus unum – out of many, one (also written as *e pluribus unum*)

Ex umbra in solem. – Out of the shade into the sunshine (said when something is explained)

Ex uno disce omnes. – From one learn all (what is true of one is true of the rest).

Ex ovis pravis non bona venit avis. From a bad egg no good bird comes.

ex scintilla incendium – from a spark a conflagration

Quid vides ex fenestra?

Hortum? Silvam? Herbam? Flores? Arbores? Domum? Canem?

Rivum? Possum? (just kidding!) Please answer in Latin!

EX-LIBRIS

PAULO JOSÉ PIRES BRANDÃO

In the olden days books were much more expensive than nowadays.

Having a collection of books at home – your own library – was a privilege.

So people put labels on their books with the words *ex libris* in Latin – from the books of...

and the name of the book owner. *Ex libris* labels often had a special emblem designed

and printed especially for the book owner and their library.

PREPOSITION *Cum*

Here is another Latin preposition for you:

cum – with, in company of

You use it with the Ablative case of nouns, just like *in, de,* and *ex.*

Discipuli cum magistra ambulant. – Students walk with the teacher.

Dominus cum domina ambulat. – Lord walks with a lady.

Domina cum domino ambulat. – Lady walks with a lord.

Domini cum dominis ambulant. – Lords walk with ladies.

Dominae cum dominis ambulant. – Ladies walk with lords.

cum grano salis – with a grain of salt

Fluvius cum mari certas. – River, you compete with the sea (*cum mari*) –

said about a person who tries to imitate someone stronger, smarter, or more important than him

pingere cum gladio – to paint with a sword (to have to come up with a clever

strategy in a difficult situation) – *gladius – gladii* n. (2) sword >> *gladiator*

OMNIA MEA MECUM PORTO.

When students earn their degrees or diplomas with honors, their diplomas say: *summa cum laude* – with highest praise, or *magna cum laude* – with great praise, or *cum laude* – with praise *laude* is the Ablative case of *laus – laudis* f. (3) *Summa cum laude* is the highest honor of all. *Summa* means 'the highest.'

The funny thing about the preposition *cum* is that it can attach itself to the end of a word! E.g., in church service they use both *cum* by itself and - *cum* attached to another word:

Dominus vobiscum. – The Lord be with you.

Et cum spiritu tuo. – And with your spirit.

Here is a popular saying with - *cum* :

Omnia mea mecum porto.

All that is mine (*omnia mea*) I carry with me

(said about talents or traits of character, as opposed to

money or material goods.)

KEEP CALM... BREATHE IN, BREATHE OUT...

- *que* = **and**

OMNIA TUA MECUM PORTO.

-QUE? TELL ME I AM DREAMING...

Cum is not the only Latin word that can attach itself to the end of another word! How about - *que* – 'and'? same as *et*, only - *que* attaches itself to the second word in the 'and' group, for example:

Marcus et Iulia = *Marcus Iuliaque*

campus et silva = *campus silvaque*

PREPOSITION *In* + Direction

Sometimes Latin prepositions can change their meaning when used with different cases. For example:

Location: *in schola* – at school – *in* + Ablative case
Direction: *in scholam* – to school – *in* + Accusative case

In schola legimus. – At school we read.
Quid in schola discis? – What are you learning at school?
Magistra in scholam venit. – Teacher comes to school.

In lecto dormio. – I sleep in bed – *lectus* m. (2)
Rex in urbem venit. – King comes to the city.
De fumo in flammam. – From smoke into flame
("out of the frying pan into the fire")

And here is another crazy, ancient verb: *ire* – to go
eo – is – it   imus – itis – eunt
Eo in scholam. – I am going to school.
For some reason verbs that are used most
are the craziest! Unfair!
Again, some nouns just don't care for the preposition *in*:
Domum eo. – I am going home.
Eo rus. – I am going to the countryside.

Proverbia et Dicta

1. *Bene dictum!* – Well said, well-put!
2. *A.M.* and *P.M.* are abbreviations for
ante meridiem – before noon and
post meridiem – after noon.
Meridiem is the Accusative case form
of the word *meridies* – noon, midday
Latin prepositions *ante* and *post*
take Accusative case.
3. *Circa* – around, about, e.g.
'circa 1800' (around year 1800),
often abbreviated to *c.*

There is a story – *fabula* – about
two Roman senators who made a bet:
Who can write the shortest letter?
The first man wrote:
Eo rus. – I'm going to the countryside.
The second man wrote:
I. – Go.
Yes, the command form of this crazy
Latin verb is *I* - just one letter!

GRAMMAR: Verbs – Command Forms

... and since I mentioned command forms, here is a simple rule about how to turn any verb into a command. Just take its infinitive form and chop off the *-re* ending:

Lege! – Read! • *Veni!* – Come! • *Dormi!* – Go to sleep!

Add *-te* if you are addressing more than one person: *Legite et discite!* – Read and learn!

Audi, vide, tace, si vis vivere in pace – Listen, watch, and be silent, if you want to live in peace.

Divide et impera! – Divide and rule! (make your enemies quarrel, so you can defeat them)

Si vis pacem, para bellum. – If you want peace, prepare for war (be ready to defend peace);

parare – to prepare

Ride si sapis. – Laugh if you are wise (= don't take things too seriously)

Lege totum si vis scire totum. – Read it all if you want to know it all (don't stop in your studies, study in-depth)

Claude os, aperi oculos! – Close your mouth, open your eyes!

> *CLAUDE OCCULOS, APERI OS!*

To tell someone not to do something, use this formula: *Noli* + infinitive of the verb

Noli dormire! – Don't sleep!

If you are addressing more than one person, make it *Nolite* + infinitive of the verb

Nolite dormire!

> *MAN, I FORGOT HOW TO MAKE A COMMAND FORM OF A VERB...*

> *R U KIDDIN' ME?*

HOMEWORK   Reading 1
Adeste Fideles Christmas Carol

The Christmas carol *Adeste Fideles*, better known as "O Come All Ye Faithful" has a bunch of verbs in a command form.

Adeste fideles laeti triumphantes,
Venite, venite in Bethlehem.
Natum videte Regem angelorum:
Venite adoremus Dominum.

adesse – to be present, to come
fidelis – faithful
triumphantes – triumphant
natus – born – native
angelus – *angeli* m. (2)
adoremus – let's worship

Reading 2 – Famous Mottos

A motto is a short sentence or a phrase that describes beliefs guiding a person, a family, or an organization. In the Middle Ages noble families in Europe had a motto written on their coat of arms (family emblem). Many organizations still have mottos. Here are a few:

Semper fidelis – the United States Marine Corps

Semper paratus – the U.S. Coast Guard

Dominus illuminatio mea – Oxford University

Deus lux mea est – Catholic University of America

Via, Veritas, Vita – University of Glasgow

Scientia est studium veritatis – Moscow University

In Deo speramus – Brown University

Veritas vos liberabit – Johns Hopkins University

Artes, scientia, veritas – University of Michigan

Lux et veritas – Yale University

Acta non verba – the United States Merchant Marine Academy

Dum spiro spero – Motto of the State of South Carolina

Scientia et sapientia – Illinois Wesleyan University

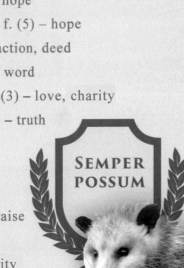

The coat of arms of Washington, D.C

And these are family mottos:

Sapientia potentia est

In veritate victoria

Lux et lex

Da mihi lucem

Fides et charitas

In veritate triumpho

Nunc aut numquam

Vincit veritas

Omnia vincit amor

Familia supra omnia

Fortes in fide

Fortis est veritas

Nil sine labore

Fidus et audax

Fides, spes, charitas

Si Deus nobiscum, qui contra nos?

Do you like my motto?

DA MIHI AQUAM

SEMPER POSSUM

potentia – *potentiae* f. (1) – power

semper – always

fides – *fidei* (f.) – faith; *fidus / fidelis* – faithful

spirare – to breathe, to hope

sperare – to hope; *spes* f. (5) – hope

actus – *actus* m. (4) – action, deed

verbum – *verbi* n. (3) – word

charitas – *charitatis* f. (3) – love, charity

veritas – *veritatis* f. (3) – truth

contra – against

vincere – to conquer

supra – above

laus – *laudis* f. (3) – praise

nil/nihil – nothing

audax – daring – audacity

Reading 3 – *Schola*

Cornelia in villa pulchra cum magno horto habitat. In hortis sunt rosae et lilia.

Cornelia in scholam venit, rosas portat et magistrae rosas dat.

Cornelia dicit: "Hoc est donum. Tibi rosas do. Te amo, quod tu es magistra mea cara."

"Tibi gratias ago," Magistra Flavia respondet. "Tu est mihi benigna."

Flavia librum Latinum tenet. "Legite!"

Nunc discipuli cum magistra legunt fabulam de silva magica. In silva magica omnes arbores argenteae sunt. In arboris argenteis aves magicae cantant. Regina silvae habet baculum magicum aureum. Sed filia reginae non est laeta.

"Cur filia reginae non laeta est?" interrogat Magistra Flavia Iulium.

"Quia unicornis albus non venit," Cornelia dicit. "Filia reginae vult amicum suum, unicornem, videre!"

"Magistra non te, sed me interrogat!" Iulius exclamat. "Possum respondere!"

"Cur unicornis venire non potest?" Magistra interrogat. "Ubi unicornis albus est?"

"Magus malus ex silva nigra venit et unicornem album capit," respondet Iulius.

"Optime. Cur capit magus unicornem?"

"Quia magus reginae inimicus est."

donum – gift – donate, donation, donor
capere (3) – to capture • ***inimicus*** – enemy
Optime! – Excellent! • ***baculum*** – wand

MEDICAL TERMS

Doctors are another profession using Latin day and night!

Look at these familiar medical terms and the Latin words they come from:

doctor – ***doctor*** m. (3) – teacher, instructor

medic, medicine – ***medicare*** (to heal)

nurse – ***nutrire*** (to nourish)

hospital – ***hospitalis*** (hospitable)

ambulance – ***ambulare*** (to walk, to move)

cure – ***curare*** (to take care of)

acute – ***acutus*** (sharp, sudden)

infection – ***inficere*** (to infect, to poison)

virus – ***virus*** (slime, poison)

dentist – ***dens*** (tooth)

cell – ***cella*** (small room)

nerve – ***nervus*** (nerve, bowstring)

abdomen – ***abdomen*** (stomach)

vertebra – ***vertebra*** (joints, vertebra)

vascular – ***vas*** (vein)

cerebral – ***cerebrum*** (brain)

osteoporosis - ***os*** (bone)

LESSON VII

Prepositions *a / ab, ad*

AHEM... ANYONE HOME?

RUN! HANNIBAL AD PORTAS!

To say 'from' in Latin, we use the preposition *a* + Ablative case;
a turns into *ab* before vowels and the letter *h* – *a casa, ab initio*.
To say 'to,' we use the preposition *ad* + Accusative case.
Magister a villa ad scholam it. – A teacher goes from house to school.
Venitne magister a schola? Non a schola venit. Unde venit magister?
A villa venit. Quo it? Ad scholam it.

In the motto of Canada *A mari usque ad mare* – From sea to sea
the Latin noun *mare – maris* n. (3) appears
in the Ablative case with the preposition *a* – *a mari*, and
in the Accusative case with the preposition *ad* – *ad mare*.
This motto comes from the Latin translation of
Psalm 72 that talks about God's rule from sea to sea –
all over the world.

ab urbe condita – from the founding
of the City. While we count years from
the birth of Jesus Christ (BC – before
Christ and AD - Anno Domini),
ancient Romans counted years from
the founding of Rome (753 BC),
for example, 20 *AUC* (*ab urbe condita*).

The motto of Colombia is
Ab ordine libertas – From order [comes] freedom
ordo – ordinis m. (3) is in the Abblative case following the preposition *ab*.

Many familiar Latin expressions use these prepositions:
A fonte puro pura defluit aqua. – From a clear spring clear water flows.
ad finem fidelis – faithful to the end
ab initio – from the beginning
ad infinitum – to infinity, forever • *ad nauseam* – too much, 'till you throw up'

HELLO?

HANNIBAL AD FENESTRAM!

ad multos annos – to many years (Latin version of "Many happy returns!")
ad victoriam – to victory (This expression was used as a battle cry by ancient Romans)
ad vitam aeternam – to eternal life, to life everlasting
Homo ad laborem natus, et avis ad volatum. – Man is born for work, and bird – for flight.
ab uno disce omnes – from one learn all
Hannibal ad portas – Hannibal is at the gate (i.e. the enemy is close)

A/ab and *ad* can be prefixes that add the meaning of 'going away / leaving' or 'coming / arriving' to a verb.

adesse = ad + esse = to be present

abesse = ab + esse = to be absent

Marcus adest, sed Claudia abest. – Marcus is present, but Claudia is absent.

Ubi timor adest, sapientia adesse nequit. – Where fear is present, wisdom is absent.

advenire = ad + venire = to arrive, to reach

Adveniat regnum tuum. – May your kingdom come (from the Lord's Prayer)

MARCUS CLAUDIUS FELIX!

ADSUM.

OLET BENE.. AMO...AMO!

If you want to ask: "What kind?" use the words

qualis (for feminine and masculine nouns)

quale (for neuter nouns).

QUALIS ROSA?

Plural: *quales* (masculine and feminine) and *qualia* (neuter)

Qualis terra est America? America terra magna et bona est.

Quales flores in horto tuo sunt? Flores albi et rubri pulchri.

If the noun is in the Accusative case, *qualis/quale* will change to the Accusative case *qualem / quale*:

Qualem librum legis? – What kind of book are you reading?

Ask me a few questions about qualities in Latin – I will answer!

What kind of trees are in the forest? **Arbores altae.**

What kind of flowers are in the field? **Flores flavi.**

What kind of stars are in the sky? **Stellae clarae.**

What kind of land is Great Britain? **Britannia insula est.**

What kind of a boy is Marcus? **Marcus est puer improbus.**

What kind of pen do you have? **Stylum aureum habeo.**

Qualis/quale are often used in proverbs and sayings:

Qualis vita, finis ita.
As your life has been,
so will be your end.
Qualis avis, talis nidus.
Like bird, like nest.

QUALES SPECTATORES? SPECTATORES LAETI SUNT.

QUALIS VIR? VIR FORTIS EST.

QUALES EQUI? EQUI ALBI SUNT.

Proverbia et Dicta

1. *quasi* – 'as if,' 'kind of'

This Latin word can be attached as a prefix to
any English word to say 'it's not quite like that, but almost,' e.g.

quasi-scientific = looks like science, but not real science

quasi-Latin = looks like Latin, but not real Latin (like Harry Potter's quasi-Latin spells)

It's a bit different from the Greek prefix *pseudo-* which means 'fake.'

Quasi- doesn't mean 'fake,' just 'similar to,' 'resembling.'

Compare: quasi-scientific = similar to science

                pseudo-scientific = fake science intended to deceive people

2. *Humanum est errare.* – People make mistakes, it's a human thing to make mistakes.

errare (1) – to make mistakes, to err – error, erratic, erroneous

3. *Caveat* means 'let him beware.' In English this word means 'a limitation,' 'a condition,'
'a suggestion.' E.g.,'I let my kid go to the party with one caveat: He must be home by 9 P.M.'

OH NO...
AM I A QUASI-BIRD?
OR A PSEUDO-FISH?

Cattus

GOVERNMENT TERMS

Many government and political terms come from Latin:

republic – *res publica* – public matters, public property

constitution – *constituere* – to set up, to arrange

government, governor – *gubernare* (1) – to guide, to rule

president – *praesidere* (2) – to guard, to govern

mayor – *major* – greater • civic, civil – *civis* citizen

cabinet – *cavea – caveae* f. (1) – a cave, an animal cage, an auditorium

Senate – *senatus – senatus* m. (4)

Congress – *congredi* – to meet, *congressus* m. (4) – a meeting

representative – *repraesentare* – to show, to show up, to pay in cash

bill – *bulla – bullae* f. (1) – a bubble, a locket necklace, a seal

veto – *vetare* (1) – to forbid; *veto* – I forbid

consensus – *consensus – consensus* m. (4) – agreement

legislative – *legis latio* (medieval Latin) – proposing/bearing law

executive – from the Latin stem *exegui* – to carry out

judicial – *jus + dicere*

federal – *foedus – foederis* n. (3) – agreement

state – from *status* – place, position

local – *locus – loci* m. (2) – place, spot

GAIUS JULIUS CAESAR

DICTATOR ROMANUS SUM!

CIVIS ROMANUS SUM!

MARCUS TULLIUS CICERO

INSECTUM ROMANUM SUM!

COCCINELLA SEPTEMPUNCTATA LINNAEUS

GRAMMAR: Accusative Case + Infinitive (*Accusativus cum Infinitivo*)

One easy way of building sentences in Latin is using the Accusative case with an infinitive of a verb –
Accusativus cum infinitivo. For example you can say:

Video canem dormire. – I see a dog sleep.

Video solem lucere. – I see the sun shine.

canem, solem – Accusative case   •   *dormire, lucere* – infinitive

In English pronouns have a 'object form' like him, her, them, us, me.

So when you say 'I hear him sing,' you are using *Accusativus cum infinitivo* in English!

You can build this type of sentence with verbs like

videre – see • *audire* – hear • *putare* – think • *scire* – know • *velle* – want   and many others.

Audio amicam meam cantare. – I hear a friend (female) sing.

Putat me bene cantare. – He/she thinks I sing well.

Videmus magistrum legere. – We see the teacher read.

Puto amicum meum laetum esse. – I think my friend is happy.

Scio me nihil scire. – I know that I know nothing (Socrates)

Est genus hominum qui volunt se esse primos omnium rerum, sed nec sunt.

There is a type of men who wish to be first in everything, and are not.

Let's make a few sentences together. Use these groups of words
to make a sentence with *Accusativus cum infinitivo*. Example:

videre – frater meus – ludere • *Video fratrem meum ludere.* I see my brother play.

videre – canis parvus – pilam capere

audire – mater mea – epistulam legere

putare – pirata – thesaurum capere

audire – avis nigra – in arbore cantare

scire – pater tuus – astronomiam docere

putare – cattus meus – computare posse

videre – amicus meus – ex fenestra spectare

SCIO NIHIL!
DISCIPULUS BONUS
NON SUM!

POSSUM

SCIO ME
NIHIL SCIRE!

SOCRATES,
PHILOSOPHUS
GRAECUS

A PSEUDO-BIRD
SINGING
A QUASI-SONG!

TWEET-TWEET!
VENITE AMICI!

HOMEWORK Translation

I walk to the forest. • You walk to the forest, but I walk to the sea.   •   I love the seashore.
(*acta – actae* f. (1) – seashore) • We walk to the seashore. • The girls often walk to the forest.
We are walking to the house.   •   They are walking to the house.   •   He is looking out of
the window.   •   I love my homeland.   •   You love the seashore but I love the forest.

Reading 1 – *Familia Romana*

Personae: Magister, Quintus (discipulus), Marcus (discipulus)

Magister: Salvete discipuli!

Quintus: Salve, magister.

Magister: Nomina vocabo. Respondete "adsum." Quintus Aurelius Flavus!

Quintus: Adsum.

Magister: Marcus Claudius Felix!

[silentium]

Magister: Marce? Marcus adest?

Quintus: Abest.

Magister: Ubi est?

Quintus [ex fenestra spectat]:

Dormit sub arbore magna illic.

Magister: Quid??? Vides Marcum dormire?

Quintus: Video et audio. Puto Marcum fessum esse.

Magister: Cur fessus est mane?

Quintus: Quia multo ludit.

Magister: O tempora! O mores! Parentibus Marci epistulam secundam scribo!

Serve! Da mihi stylum et tabulam! [scribit] Porta epistulam meam Claudio, patri Marci.

Quintus [sub arbore magna]: Marce! Marce! Veni! Magister iratus est!

Marcus: Nolo discere! Volo dormire!

vocabo – will call

sub + Acc. case – under

fessus – tired

mane – in the morning, early

serve – address form (Vocative Case) of

servus servi m. (1) – servant, slave

porta – command form of *portare*

veni – command form of *venire*

iratus – angry

Reading 2 – *Schola*

Magistra Flavia fabulam magicam discipulis legit. Discipuli audiunt. Magistra picturas ostendit.
Discipuli spectant. Filiae reginae silvae nomen Aemilia est. Aemilia librum magicum aureum habet.
Dicit Aemilia libro: "Ostende mihi ubi unicornis meus est in pagina prima!"
Et vidit Aemilia librum unicornem in prima pagina ostendere, et audit Aemilia unicornem plorare!
"Ubi es, amice care, unicornis?" Ea interrogat.
Sed tacit unicornis albus, nil dicit. Non potest dicere. Vidit Aemilia unicornem in silvam nigram
esse. Vidit magum malum cum baculo magico nigro in silva sub arbores nigras sedere et ridere!
"Habeo unicornem tuum!" dicit magus. "Vis unicornem habere? Veni ad silvam nigram! Te expecto!"
"Non te timeo, mage," Aemilia dicit. "Possum te vincere et magiam nigram tuam delere!"
"Hahaha! Immo, non credo," ridet magus malus.
Magus baculum magicum suum tenet. "Nox!" dicit. Venit nox in silvam nigram.
"Potes noctem delere?" Magus interrogat et ridet.
"Velle est posse," Aemilia respondet.

ostendere (3) – to show – ostentatious
expectare – to expect
pagina – paginae f. (1) – page
primus – first – prime • *nil* – nothing
Velle est posse – to want is to be able
("Where there is a will, there is a way.")

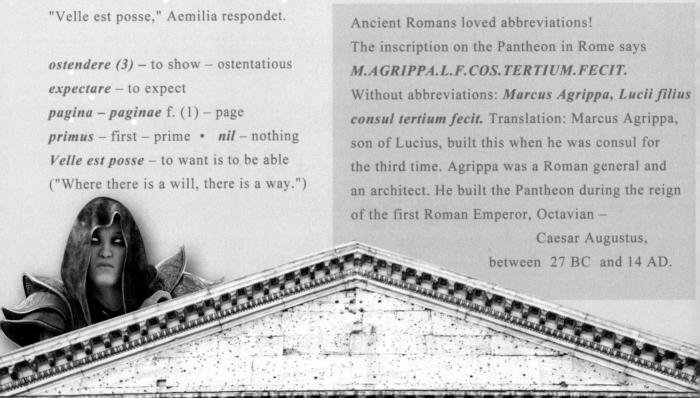

Ancient Romans loved abbreviations!
The inscription on the Pantheon in Rome says
M.AGRIPPA.L.F.COS.TERTIUM.FECIT.
Without abbreviations: ***Marcus Agrippa, Lucii filius***
consul tertium fecit. Translation: Marcus Agrippa,
son of Lucius, built this when he was consul for
the third time. Agrippa was a Roman general and
an architect. He built the Pantheon during the reign
of the first Roman Emperor, Octavian –
Caesar Augustus,
between 27 BC and 14 AD.

M·AGRIPPA·L·F·COS·TERTIVM·FECIT

LESSON VIII

GRAMMAR: Verbs – Past Imperfect Tense and Past Perfect Tense

So far we've used verbs only in the present tense: she says, he writes, etc. Let's start learning about past and future tenses. There are a few tenses in Latin, but we'll go one step at a time.

First, we'll take our ancient, crazy verb *esse* – to be, and study its forms in past tense.

	I am	you are	he/she/it/is	we are	you (pl.) are	they are
Present:	*sum*	*es*	*est*	*sumus*	*estis*	*sunt*
	I was	you were	he/she/it/was	we were	you (pl.) were	they are
Past:	*eram*	*eras*	*erat*	*eramus*	*eratis*	*erant*

All the endings sound familiar, right? But the consonants change in the middle of the verb.

That happens even with regular verbs that are not as ancient and crazy as *esse*. *Esse* is used so often, though, that we should be familiar with its forms for sure. For example, here is the beginning of the Gospel of John in Latin:

In principio erat Verbum et Verbum erat apud Deum et Deus erat Verbum.

In the beginning was the Word, and the Word was with God, and the Word was God.

A couple more examples:

Sic semper erat, et sic semper erit. This is how it has always been, and this is how it shall ever be.

In Foro Romano templa multa et splendida erant.

In the Forum of Rome (*Forum Romanum*) there were many beautiful temples.

OK, now let's take a regular verb and see what forms it has in past tense...

But first, let me say this: Past and future tenses of Latin verbs may be tricky, but our goal is not to use these verbs in fluent Latin conversation. Our goal is to be able to recognize these verbs in written text. So don't worry about memorizing stuff. Just notice the suffixes and the endings used to form past tense and see if you can tell the tense of the verb when it appears in a sentence.

Just like in English we can say: "I did" and "I have done," "I wrote" and "I have written," so in Latin, too, we have different ways of talking about the past. We have

Past Perfect (1-time action) – 'I have written a letter' –

Scripsi epistulam.

and Past Imperfect (repeated or continued for some time) – I wrote letters. / I was writing...–

Scribebam epistulas.

Here are the most common endings of Latin verbs for these two types of past tense:

Imperfect Past tense endings:

I ...	you...	he/she/it...	we...	you ...	they....
- bam	*- bas*	*- bat*	*- bamus*	*- batis*	*- bant*

Perfect Past Tense endings:

	I ...	you...	he/she/it...	we...	you ...	they....
Past:	*-i*	*- isti*	*- it*	*- imus*	*- istis*	*- erunt*

Imperfect Past   *narrabam fabulas* – I told stories

                narrabas fabulas – you told stories

                narrabat fabulas – he/she told stories

                narrabamus fabulas – we told stories

                narrabatis fabulas – you (more than 1) told stories

                narrabant fabulas – they told stories

Perfect Past   *narravi fabulam* – I've told a story

                narravisti fabulam – you've told a story

                narravit fabulam – he/she's told a story

                narravimus fabulam – we've told a story

                narravistis fabulam – you've (more than 1) told...

                narraverunt fabulam – they've told a story

Latin is a language
Dead as dead can be.
It killed the ancient Romans,
And now it's killing me.

Examples:

Veni, vidi, vici. – These words were said by Julius Caesar who reported to the Roman Senate that he 'came, saw, and defeated' his enemy. These words are the Past Perfect tense forms of:

venire, videre, vincere

Caesar used Past Perfect tense, because 'came, saw, and defeated' were one-time actions.

Romani multos deos adorabant. – Romans worshipped many gods.

In this sentence we have the Past Imperfect tense of the verb *adorare* – to adore, to worship.

The use of Past Imperfect tense indicates that worshipping many gods was not a one-time action – this is something Romans used to do all the time.

Olim in Lydia regnabat rex, Croesus nomine.

Long ago, in Lydia, there reigned a king, Croesus by name. – Again, Past Imperfect tense tells us that 'reigned' was not a one-time action – it continued for some years.

Christus nos liberavit. – Christ freed/liberated us. One-time action >> Past Perfect tense

Quid magister vos docuit hodie? – What has the teacher taught you today?

This sentence uses Past Perfect tense – 'has taught,' not 'was teaching,' or 'taught,' because the action has started and has ended. Compare *docuit* – 'has taught' with *docet* – 'teaches.'

In the Past Perfect tense most verbs change consonants in their stem, usually adding *v* or *u* to the main portion of the word – before the ending.

doc changes its stem to *docu* – I have taught – *docui* – You have taught - *docuisti*

amare changes its stem to *amav* – I have loved – *amavi* –You have loved – *amavisti*

ambulare changes its stem to *ambulav* – *Ambulavi in silva.* – I have gone for a walk in the woods.

narrare changes its stem to *narrav* – *Narravit me fabulam.* – He/she told me a story.

Some verbs have *s* or *x* added to their stem in the Past Perfect:

scribere – scripsi (I have written)

dicere – dixi (I have said)

lucere – luxi (I have shined light)

Read the sentences below and figure out if
the verb is in Past Imperfect or Past Perfect tense:

Puella audivit fabulam.

Discipuli magistrum salutaverunt.

Amicis meis credebam.

Spectavimus canem ludere.

Portavi aquam ad casam.

Fratri mei in schola discebant.

Magister fabulam narravit.

With some verbs, some present-tense forms
look exactly like past-tense forms, for example:

venit – he/she comes • *venit* – he/she came

legit – he/she reads • *legit* – he/she has read.

When Latin was a spoken language, in the days
of *Roma Antiqua*, these forms were pronounced
differently. In one form *e* was a long vowel,
in the other form *e* was pronounced as a short vowel.

Magister dixit.
In the Middle Ages scholars were in awe of
Aristotle, one of the greatest philosophers
of Ancient Greece (*Graecia Antiqua*).
During scholarly discussions, if one of the
scholars managed to come up with a quote
from Aristotle, the discussion was over.
Aristotle's opinion was the last word, and
it was usually announced with the words:
Magister dixit – The teacher has said it.

Pinxit.
In the Middle Ages and during the era of the Renaissance artists often
signed their paintings with the word *Pinxit* + their name. *Pinxit* is
the Past Perfect tense form of the verb *pingere* – to paint.
Picturam pinxi. I painted a picture. Sometimes artists used abbreviations *P, PIN* or *PINX.*

UNIVERSITY TERMS

If you want to be bombarded with Latin, go to college!

Take a look at these words used in every single college and university!

education – *educatio – educationis* f. (3) – training, bringing up

college – *collegium – collegii* n. (3) – society, college

university – *universitas – universitatis* f. (3) – gathering

curriculum – *curriculum curriculi* n. (2) – race, running, course, chariot race

vacation – *vacare* (1) – to be empty, to be free

course – *cursus – cursus* m. (4) running, race

student – *studium – studii* m. (2) – study

professor – *profiteri* – to claim, to declare, to profess

lecture – *legere* (3) – to read

colloquium – *colloqui* – to discuss

seminar – *seminare* (1) – to plant, to sow

exam – *examinare* (1) – to test, to weigh, to examine

grade – *gradus – gradus* m. (4) – step, position

class – *classis – classis* f. (3) – group

graduation – *gradi* – to walk, to step

diploma – *diploma – diplomatis* n. (3) – a letter of recommendation

B.A. – Bachelor of Arts – *artium baccalaureus* (from *baculum* – staff)

M.A. – Master of the Arts – *artium magister*

Ph.D. or D.Phil. – Doctor of Philosophy – *Philosophiae Doctor*

dissertation – *dissertatio – dissertationis* f. (3) – discourse

alma mater – 'nurturing mother,' one's university

Proverbia et Dicta

1. *Fidem qui perdit, perdere ultra nil potest.* – He who lost faith has nothing more to lose.

perdere – to lose, to destroy; *ulter (ulterior, ultimus)* – adjective – that is beyond

2. *Mali principii, malus finis.* – Bad principles, bad results (bad foundations, bad ending).

principii – beginnings, foundations, principles

3. *Ave Caesar, morituri te salutant!* – Hail, Emperor, those who are about to die salute you.

morituri – those who are going to die.

According to Roman historian Suetonius, these were the words of Roman gladiators arriving to fight in the arena of the Roman Colosseum. Gladiators were prisoners of war or criminals forced to fight to the death at a circus to entertain the Roman public.

The word *gladiator* comes from *gladius – gladii* n. (2) – sword

Reading 1 – *Familia Romana*

Personae: Marcus (puer), Valeria (mater)

Marcus plorat.

Valeria: Fili mi care, cur plores?

Marcus: Quintus me pulsavit!

Valeria: Quintus puer malus est! Viditne magister eum te pulsare? Cur te pulsavit?

Marcus: Quia eum pulsavi... uhu-hu-hu

Valeria: Quid? Cur eum pulsavisti?

Marcus: Dixit quod piger sum!

Valeria: Quintus puer improbus! Audivitne magister? Cur dixit Quintus quod piger es?

Marcus: Quia magister dixit quod piger sum!

Valeria: OMJ! (Oh My Jupiter) Di immortales! Cur?

Marcus: Quia non eum audivi, sed dormivi...

Reading 2 – *Schola*

Magistra discipulis fabulam magicam legit.

Vesper erat. Aemilia, filia reginae, sola ad silvam nigram in terra incognita ambulabat. Procul silva, et via longa erat. In terra incognita fluvius niger frigidus fluebat et bestiae feroces habitabant. Nubes in caelo, luna et stellae obscurae erant. Aemilia non laeta, tristis erat. Ea de unicorne suo putabat et plorabat. Cum venit Aemilia in silvam nigram, nox erant. Aemilia viam non videbat. In silva audivit Aemilia vocem magi mali, sed magum non spectavit.

"Nana-nana-na!" magus risit. "Nil vides! Unicornem tuum invenire non potes!"

Habebat Aemilia rosam rubram, donum matris suae. Illa rosa magica erat. Portavit Aemilia rosam in silvam nigram.

"Rosa, da mihi lucem!" Aemilia dixit. Lux magna alba ex rosa luxit. Vidit Aemilia magum malum in arbore nigro sedere et unicornem album sub arboro stare! Vocavit Aemilia unicornem: "Veni, amice!"

Unicornis vidit magum, baculum magicum magi cepit, et cum Aemilia ex silva nigra exivit!

fili – address form (Vocative case) of *filius*

mi/mei – address form of *meus* – my

pulsare (1) – to hit, to beat – pulse, pulsate

eum – him

Di immortales! – Immortal gods!

QUINTUS ME PULSAVIT!

tristis – sad

incognitus – unknown – incognito

procul – far away

fluere – to flow

cum – when

invenire – to find, to discover – invent

risit – Past Perfect of *ridere* – to laugh

stare – to stand – static

vocare – to call

amice – address form of *amicus* – friend

cepit – he/she captured (from *capere* – to grasp, to capture)

exire – to exit

LESSON IX

HODIE CATTUS SUM.
CRAS LEO ERO!

GRAMMAR: Verbs – Future Imperfect Tense

In this lesson we'll learn the Latin Future Imperfect tense. Just like in the Past Imperfect, the Future Imperfect action does not have a distinctive beginning or end – it's just going to happen sometime in the future and probably continue for some time or repeat.

Let's start with our favorite verb *esse* – to be. Let's compare its forms in Present, Past, and Future:

	I am	you are	he/she/it/is	we are	you (pl.) are	they are
Present:	*sum*	*es*	*est*	*sumus*	*estis*	*sunt*
	I was	you were	he/she/it/was	we were	you (pl.) were	they are
Past:	*eram*	*eras*	*erat*	*eramus*	*eratis*	*erant*
	I'll be	you'll be	he/she/it'll be	we'll be	you (pl.) will be	they'll be
Future:	*ero*	*eris*	*erit*	*erimus*	*eritis*	*erunt*

Ubi cras eris? – Where will you be tomorrow? *Cras in schola ero.* – Tomorrow I'll be at school.
Ubi cras eritis? – Where will you (more than one person) be tomorrow?
Cras domi erimus. – Tomorrow we'll be at home.

Adde parvum parvo magnus acervus erit. - Add a little to a little, and there will be a big heap.
Non semper erit aestas. – It will not always be summer.
Qui non est hodie, cras minus aptus erit. –
The one who is not prepared (aptus) today will be less prepared tomorrow.
Tristis eris, si solus eris. – You will be sad, if you are alone.

NESCIO QUID CRAS ERO. CENA AVIS?

Let's make a few sentences with *esse* in Present, Past, and Future. I'll make a sentence starting with *hodie* – 'today,' and you will change my sentence to past tense and start it with *heri* – 'yesterday,' and then you will change it to future tense and start it with *cras* – 'tomorrow.'

Hodie in schola sum. Today I am at school. *Heri... Cras...*
Hodie laeta/laetus sum. Today I am happy. *Heri... Cras...*
Hodie magistra sum. Today I am a teacher. *Heri... Cr...*

HERI OVUM ERAM. CRAS GALLINA ERO.

Ok, enough of the crazy *esse*! What about other – normal! – verbs?

Easy! Compare: Present: **Sol lucet.** – The sun is shining.

Future: **Sol lucebit.** – The sun will shine.

Present: **Computo.** – I count.

Future: **Computabo.** – I will count.

Speech bubble: *CRAS DISCAM. HODIE DORMIO. ZZZZZ.*

SCHOLA

To form Future Imperfect tense you add suffix - **ba** + ending to a verb stem

Verbs of the 1st and 2nd conjugations – Future Imperfect endings:

I ...	you...	he/she/it...	we...	you ...	they....
- **bo**	- **bis**	- **bit**	- **bimus**	- **bitis**	- **bunt**

Verbs of the 3rd and 4th conjugations – Future Imperfect endings:

I ...	you...	he/she/it...	we...	you ...	they....
- **am**	- **es**	- **et**	- **emus**	- **etis**	- **ent**

Examples:

amare (1)

Speech bubble: *AMABO TE AETERNUM.*

Future Imperfect tense: *amabo – amabis – amabit*

amabimus – amabitis – amabunt

scribere (3)

Future Imperfect tense: *scribam – scribes – scribet*

scribemus – scribetis – scribent

audire (4)

ACTA

Future Imperfect tense: *audiam – audies – audiet*

audiemus – audietis – audient

Quis separabit nos? – Who will divide us? *separare* (1) – to divide, to separate

Qui quae vult dicit, quod non vult audiet.

He who says [only] what he wants, will hear what he doesn't want [to hear.]

Dominus providebit – The Lord will provide – *providere* (2) – to provide for, to foresee

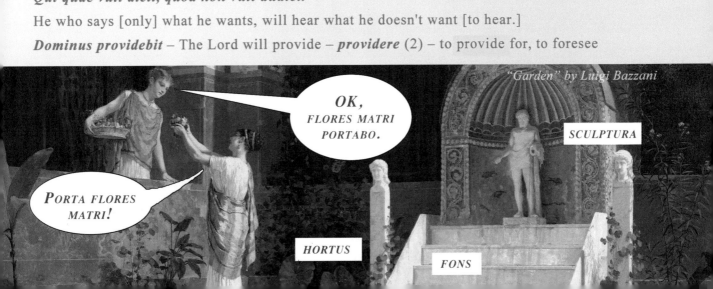

"Garden" by Luigi Bazzani

Speech bubble: *OK, FLORES MATRI PORTABO.*

SCULPTURA

Speech bubble: *PORTA FLORES MATRI!*

HORTUS

FONS

GRAMMAR: Past Participle

A verbal form very useful in both English and Latin is the past participle, like 'said,' 'tied,' 'seen,' 'done,' 'gone,' etc. A participle is part verb and part adjective. It is typically used with the verb 'to be' in English: 'He was seen. She is gone.' Same in Latin!

Amatus sum. – I was loved.

Unicornis captus est. – The unicorn was captured.

Past Participles end in either - *tum* (as in *amatum*) or - *sum* (as in *missum*). Because participles are so much like adjectives, they echo the endings of nouns, just like adjectives do. E.g.:

Verbum dictum est. – The word was said.

P.S. – post scriptum – a comment added at the end of a letter, article, or book

Fabula narrata est. – The story was told.

Multae fabulae narratae sunt. – Many stories were told.

Doctus est. – He was taught (He is a learned man.)

docta ignorantia – learned ignorance (said about educated people who make poor choices)

Nihil scriptum est. – Nothing was/is written.

Ita lex scripta. – Such is the law.

Filius meus decem annos natus est. – My son is 10 years old ('natus est' = was born).

Dicta tibi est lex. – The law has been laid down (said) for you.

Dictum de dicto. – Said from what was said (a report based on hearsay)

Alea iacta est. – 'The die has been cast.' According to the Roman historian Suetonius, these were the words said by Julius Caesar as he led his army across the Rubicon river.

iacta is the past participle formed from the verb *iacere* – to throw, to cast

Acta est fabula. Plaudite! – 'The play is done. Applaud!' These words were usually said at the end of a play in Roman theaters. Suetonius wrote that these were also the last words of Emperor Caesar Augustus. *Acta* is the past participle formed from the verb *agere* (3) – to act

Gratis dictum – said 'for free' (when someone says something unrelated to the conversation)

dictum is the past participle formed from the verb *dicere* – to say

Multi sunt vocati, pauci vero electi. Many are called but few are chosen (from the Gospel of Matthew 22:14).

Bene nati, bene vestiti, et mediocriter docti. – Well-born, well-dressed, and given a mediocre education (poorly taught). *Doctus – docti* – taught, from *docere* – to teach

lex non scripta – an unwritten law

Verba volant, scripta manent. – Spoken words fly away, what is written remains.

Many English words of Latin origin are formed from the Latin Past Participles. For example:

legere – to read – Past Participle: *lectum* >> lecture

agere – to act – Past Participle: *actum* >> action, active, actual

mittere – to send – Past Participle: *missum* >> mission, dismiss, emission, omission, permission

Verbum emissum non est revocabile. – A word once spoken cannot be recalled.

omissis iocis – leaving joking aside

committere – to connect, to commit, to put together – Past Participle: *commissum* >> commission

pati – to suffer – Past Participle: *passum* >> passion, passive

convincere – to convince – Past Participle: *convictum* >> conviction

> *OMISSIS IOCIS, QUIS ES?*

The word 'mass' – Catholic church service – also comes from

mittere – missum – to send

The mass usually ends with this dialogue between the priest and the people:

Priest: *Dominus vobiscum.* – The Lord be with you.

People: *Et cum spiritu tuo.* – And with your spirit.

Priest: *Ite, missa est.* – Go. It is over ('It has been sent.')

People: *Deo gratias.* – Thanks be to God.

Proverbia et Dicta

1. *non sequitur* – 'it doesn't follow' – an inconsistent statement
2. *Vincit qui se vincit.* – He conquers who conquers himself.
3. *Vox clamantis in deserto* – a voice crying in the wilderness

This phrase is used in the gospels to refer to John the Baptist who preached the coming of Jesus Christ. It has been used as a motto. For example, it's the motto of Dartmouth College. In modern English the expression means 'someone whose idea or opinion is ignored, not popular.'

PREPOSITION *Per*

And now let's learn one more Latin preposition widely used in modern English – *per.*

Per means by, through, by means of and it is used with the Accusative case of nouns. Examples:

per se – by itself

Per deos! – By the gods! (exclamation of surprise)

per mare, per terras – by sea and by land (lands)

Qui per virtutem peritat, non interit. – He who dies for virtue, does not perish.

LATIN BUSINESS TERMS

Many terms used in business and accounting also come from Latin!

cost – *constare* (1) – to be fixed, to stand still

cash – **capsa** – **capsae** f. (1) – box, container

percent – *per centum* – by the hundred

profit – *proficere* (3) – to succeed, to profit

account – *a + computare*

asset – *ad satis* = till sufficient

revenue – *re- + venire*

transaction – *transactio* – *transactionis* f. (3) – agreement, deal

debt, debit – **debere** (2) – to owe, *debitum debiti* n. (2) – what is owed

credit card – *credere* – to believe, *creditum* – loan; card << *carrere* (3) – to comb, clean

per annum – by the year, yearly • Example: 'My per annum income is $100,000.'

per diem – by the day • Example: 'My per diem expenses are $100' (what you spend each day).

per capita = 'for each head,' or for each person *caput* – *capitis* n. (3) – head; plural: *capita*

Example: income *per capita* – approximate income for one person in a country/city etc.

'Money' comes from *Moneta* – a title of the Roman goddess Juno near whose temple they coined money in Rome. Moneta << *monere* – to advise, to admonish a god/goddess

Lots of familiar English words come from the Latin *caput*: chapter, capital, capitol, decapitate, capital punishment. 'Capitulate' comes from *capitula* – little/reduced heading/chapter (insufficient, bad terms)

REVENUE MINUS EXPENSES EQUALS PROFIT!

EMPEROR AUGUSTUS MAKES GREAT SPEECHES IN LATIN! BRAVO!

DEBIT SHOULD NOT EXCEED CREDIT! OR... DECAPITATE!

HOMEWORK

Translation

Where were you yesterday? I was at home (*domi*).

And where are you today? Today I am at my country house (*villa rustica mea*).

And where will you be tomorrow? Tomorrow I will be in town (*in urbe*).

My friends were in the garden (*in horto*) yesterday, but tomorrow they'll be in the woods (*in silvis*).

Yesterday my the teacher was at home (*domi*), but tomorrow he will be at school (*in schola*).

The book was read (*legere* – Past Participle masculine: *lectus*)

The voice (*vox* f.(3)) of the king was heard (*audire* – Past Participle feminine: *audita*).

ROMAN INSCRIPTIONS

The Arch of Titus was built in Rome to commemorate the conquest of Judaea in AD 71. It is dedicated to Emperor Titus.

SENATUS POPULUSQUE ROMANUS
DIVO TITO DIVI VESPASIANI F.VESPASIANO AUGUSTO.

The Senate and the people of Rome –
to Divine Titus Vespasian Augustus,
son of Divine Vespasian

Divo Tito Vespasiano Augusto, filio – Dative Case

Divi Vespasiani – Genitive Case (of Divine Vespasian)

Senatus Populusque Romanus was often abbreviated to *S.P.Q.R.* These letters appeared on Roman military standards, and Roman soldiers had *SPQR* tattoos.

The inscription from the Emperor Trajan's monument in Rome:
'S.P.Q.R. to the Emperor,
son of Caesar Nerva,
Trajan, the best ruler'

Reading – *Familia Romana*

Personae: Marcus (puer), Claudius (pater)

Claudius [iratus, tenet epistulam]: O Iupiter! Marce! Tecum colloqui volo.

Magister epistulam secundam scripsit:

> Magister Claudii salutem dicit. Si vales, bene est; ego valeo. Discipulus piger est tuus filius. Hodie tabulam et stylum non portavit, et – horribile dictu! – fabulam Aesopi *Vulpes et Uva* non legit. In via ad ruinam filius tuus est. Disce aut discede! Vale.

Claudius: Dicta tibi est lex, Marce. Magister tuus doctus est, vir benignus est. Sed non vis discere! 'Disce aut discede,' Magister dixit. Ergo ab hoc die non ludes, sed in campo laborabis!

Marcus: O me miserum! Pater, ero discipulus bonus! Ab hoc die discam bene, legam fabulas Aesopi de vulpibus et ceteris animalibus! Computabo multo, et tabulam semper portabo, et scribam pulchre!

Claudius: Quid audio? Non tibi credo! Scio quod male disces, computabis, et scribes, et fabulas non leges! Ab hoc die in campo cum porcis laborabis! Experientia docet.

Marcus: Nolo in campo cum porcis esse! Humanum est errare!

Claudius: Vere dicis.

Marcus: Quintus discipulus malus quoque est, sed in campo non laborabit!

Claudius: In latrina laborabit Quintus! Scio patrem suum iratum esse!

Marcus: Hmmm... [putat] Melius cum porcis quam in latrina laborare... Excusa me, pater... Possum in culina quoque laborare!

---

colloqui – to talk

horribile dictu! – horrible to tell!

Vulpes et Uva – the Fox and the Grapes

via ad ruinam – the road to ruin

Disce aut discede! – Learn or leave!

benignus – nice, benign

ergo – therefore

ab hoc die – from this day on

ludere Imperfect Future:

ludam – ludes – ludet

ludemus – ludetis– ludent

labore Imperfect Future:

laborabo – laborabis – laborabit

laborabimus – laborabitis – laborabunt

O me miserum! – O wretched me!

Humanum est errare! – to err is human

semper – always

porcus – porci m. (2) – pig – pork

Excusa me – Excuse me

Experientia docet. – Experience teaches.

latrina – latrinae f. (1) – toilet

culina – culinae f. (1) – kitchen – culinary

melius – better

quam – than

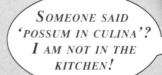

SOMEONE SAID 'POSSUM IN CULINA'? I AM NOT IN THE KITCHEN!

LESSON X

GRAMMAR: Instrumental Ablative Case = 'by / with'

Think of English prepositional phrases like 'by law,' 'by force,' 'by chance,' or 'with' phrases – 'writing with a pen,' 'cutting with a knife.' These 'by' and 'with' phrases can be translated into Latin with an Ablative case form of a noun – without any preposition! This is known as *Ablativus Instrumentalis* – Instrumental Ablative case.

jure divino – by divine law; *jure humano* – by human law; Ablative of *jus – uris* n. (3) – right, law

Plumbo nomen tuum scribe, quaeso. – Write down your name with a pencil, please.

una voce – with one voice, unanimously; Abblative case of *vox – voxis* f. (3)

bona fide – in good faith, Ablative case of – *fides – fidei* f. (5) – faith

non gladio, sed gratia – not by the sword but by good will.

Abblative of *gladius – gladii* n. (2) and *gratia* f. (1) – grace, good will

rex Croesus nomine – king by the name of Croesus, 'king Croesus by name,' Abl. of *nomen* n.

Please translate into Latin: I write with a pen. • A king wins (*vincere* (3)) with a sword.
A philosopher (*philosophus* m. (2)) wins with a word (*verbum* n. (2)).
I said (*dixi*) what I said in good faith.

LATIN TERMS IN COMPUTER SCIENCE

digital – *digitus – digiti* m. (2) – finger • The idea of digit=numeral comes from counting on fingers!

computer – *computare* (1) – to count, calculate

monitor – *monitor – monitoris* m. (3) – a guide, an advisor

processor – *procedere* – go forward (*processus* = Past Participle)

memory – *memoria – memoriae* f. (1)

remote – *remotus* – distant

interface – *inter* = between, *facies – faciei* f. (5) – appearance

application – *applicare* (1) – to connect

artificial intelligence – *artificialis* – artful, *intellegere* – understand

data – *datum* – given, Past Participle of *dare* – to give

file – *filum – fili n. (2)* – a string, a filament, a thread of fate

virtual reality – *virtus* – excellence, manliness + *realis* – real

malware – prefix *mal-* comes from *malus* – bad

media – *medium – medii* n. (2) – middle

A Nile Monitor lizard was believed to warn people of Nile crocodiles, that's why they named it *monitor* = advisor, guide

GRAMMAR: Adjectives – Comparative and Superlative Degrees

In English, to compare qualities of objects we use the Comparative and Superlative degrees of adjectives. For example: *high* • Comparative degree: *higher* • Superlative degree: *the highest*

In Latin we have the same three degrees of adjectives!!

To form Comparative degrees, use suffixes

- *ior* for masculine and feminine nouns

- *ius* for neuter nouns

To form Superlative degrees, use suffixes

- *issimus, - issima, - issimum*

clarus – bright, *clarior* – brighter, *clarissimus* – the brightest

brevis – short, *brevior* – shorter, *brevissimus* – the shortest

velox – fast, *velocior* – faster, *velocissimus* – the fastest

> HEY CAESAR, JOIN OUR DANCE COMPETITION! VENI, VIDE, ET VINCE!

> HMMM... PESSIMUS SALTATOR SUM.

Many famous mottos and Latin sayings use Comparative and Superlative degrees of adjectives.

Fama nihil est celerius. – Nothing is faster than a rumor (Abl. case of *fama*)

celer – fast, *celerius* – faster – accelerate, acceleration

Quid dulcius homini a natura datum est, quam sui liberi?

What has been given by nature more dear to man than his children?

Quid leone fortius? – Who is braver than a lion? (Abl. case of *leo*)

The word *excelsior* used in a lot of mottos means "higher" – from *excelsus* – high

The motto of the Olympic games uses three comparative degrees:

Citius, Altius, Fortius – Faster, Higher, Stronger

> FLOS ALBISSIMUS

'A Dancer' by Gugliemo Zocchi

> OPTIMA SALTATRIX!

> BONA SALTATRIX!

> BENE SALTAS!

> GRATIAS! AMO SALTARE!

As always, some of most widely used adjectives end up totally irregular! At least it's easy to remember these irregular forms because many English adjectives came from them:

bonus – good, *melior* – better, *optimus* – the best
>>> English: ameliorate (to improve something), optimal (the best)
Melior est avis in manu quam decem in aere. – Better one bird in hand than ten in the air.
Vir sapiens forti melior. – A wise man is better than a strong one.
magnus – big, *maior* – bigger, *maximus* – the biggest
>>> English: major, maximum, maxim (a wise saying)
Ubi major pars est, ibi est totum. – Where the greater part is, there is the whole.
In maxima fortuna minima licentia est. – In the greatest fortune there is least freedom.
malus – bad, *peior* – worse, *pessimus* – the worst
>>> English: pejorative (negative), pessimistic (hopeless)
Corruptio optimi pessima. – The corruption of the best is the worst.
multus – much, *plus* – more, *plurimus* – most
>>> English: plus, plural
parvus – small, *minor, minus* – smaller, *minimus* – the smallest
>>> English: minor, minus, minimum, minimal, minimalist
ulter – *ulterior* – *ultimus* – the last, the most extreme – ultimatum, ultra- (prefix)
ultimus Romanorum – the last of the Romans
exterus – outward, *exterior* – outer, further out, *extremus* – outermost, last
>>> English: exterior, extreme, extremist
inferus – low, *inferior* – lower, *infimus* – the lowest
>>> English: inferior, inferiority
posterus – next, *posterior* – later, *postumus* – last
>>> English: posterior, posthumous
superus – above, *superior* – higher, *supremus/summus* – highest
>>> English: superior, superiority, supreme, sum, summary
Summa sedes non capit duos. –
The highest seat does not hold two.

Can you believe this? Practically every form of these adjectives is used in modern English! Hurray for Latin!

MINIMUM SUM.

ANTIQUISSIMA SUM.

WOW, PISCIS MAXIMUS!

S-s-s-s-s-s-s!

LONGIOR SUM.

PREPOSITION *Inter*

Ok, here comes one more Latin preposition you know well – *inter*!

inter = between, among + Accusative case

inter alia – among other things • *inter nos* – between us

princeps inter pares – the first among equals (leader chosen by his equals)

cygnus inter anates – a swan among ducks

Inter also appears as a prefix in many words. That's where international, intercontinental, and intergalactic come from.

Many English words are formed using Latin prepositions/prefixes.
Let's take the Latin word *cedere* – 'to make way,' and see what English words come from it in combination with various Latin prefixes:

pro – for, before, forth >> proceed, process, procession

pre – before >> precede, preceding, precedent

sub/su – under, close to >> succeed, success

inter – between >> intercede (to step in to help or defend someone)

e/ex – out, from >> exceed (go over), excessive

re =– back >> recede (step back), recess

cum/con/co – with, together >> concede (yield, stop fighting), concession

pre – before + *de* (about, from) >> predecessor

se – apart >>secede (separate, break away)

Another example: *vox – vocis* f. (3)

e/ex – out, from >> evoke (bring out emotion or memory), evocative

in – in, to >> invoke (call, mention), invocation

pro – for, before, forth >> provoke

re – back >> revoke (to cancel)

> THIS RECESSION EVOKES A PRECEDENT OF SECESSION AND VICE VERSA!

> I'LL INTERCEDE TO REVOKE PRECEDING PROCESS DURING RECESS!

> THIS EXCESSIVE PROCESSION PROVOKES CONCESSION!

> RECEDE AND CONCEDE, SO I CAN PROCEED AND SUCCEED! AND ET CETERA.

> EMPEROR TRAJAN MAKES SPECTACULAR SPEECHES IN LATIN! WOW!

> QUID DICIT? IS HE OK?

Proverbia et Dicta

1. *vice versa* – the other way around • 2. *sic* – so, 'quoted exactly as it appears in the original'

3. *Aut Caesar, aut nullus.* – Either Caesar, or nobody – or *Aut Caesar, aut nihil.* – Either Caesar, or nothing. It's a saying based on the words of Julius Caesar "I'd rather be first in a faraway village than second in Rome."

HOMEWORK Reading 1 – *Montes et Fluvii Americae*

Denali mons altus est, altior quam ceteri montes Americae. Is mons Americae altissimus est.
Missouri fluvius longus est, longior quam ceteri fluvii Americae. Is fluvius longissimus est.
America habet montes altiores et fluvii longiora quam Anglia.

Reading 2 – *Multa Proverbia et Dicta*

Read these Latin sayings and come up with a short dialog showing how you could use one of these
sayings in a conversation. For example: My friend Katie gives me an early birthday gift,
and I say to her *Bis dat qui cito dat!*

Maximum miraculum homo sapiens.

Bis dat qui cito dat.

Bis vivit qui bene vivit.

Domus amica, domus optima.

Crede quod habes, et habes.

Damnant quod non intellegunt.

Deus est summum bonum.

Felix qui nihil debet.

Fortes fortuna adjuvat.

Homo homini aut deus aut lupus.

In aqua scribis.

In arena aedificas.

terra firma

Nil dictum quod non dictum prius.

Quem Iupiter vult perdere, dementat prius.

Quid male agit odit lucem.

Qui non est aptus hodie, cras minus aptus erit.

Qui non laborat, non manducet.

Res, non verba.

Tempus omnia revelat.

Tempus omnia terminat.

Ubi amici, ibi opes.

Veritas odium parit.

Vir sapiens forti melior.

Virtus vincit invidiam.

Vivat rex!

Vive valeque!

via media

alter ego

Vide et crede!

Aut vincere aut mori.

Adversus miseros inhumanus est iocus.

Fortuna caeca est.

Nemo dat quod non habet.

Nemo malus felix.

Magis mutus quam piscis.

Manus manum lavat.

Qualis pater, talis filius.

tabula rasa

Ubi amor, ibi fides.

Unus vir, nullus vir.

TESLA MELIOR EST!

TOYOTA PRIUS

SHHH! MAGIS MUTUS QUAM…

DID SOMEONE JUST SAY 'NEMO'?

aedeficere – to build – edifice

adjuvare – to help, to encourage

adversus – against – adversary

alter – other – alter, alternate, alternative

amicus (adjective) – friendly – amicable

aptus – prepared, ready – apt, aptitude

arena – *arenae* f. (1) – sand

bis – twice

caecus – blind

cito – fast, without delay

cupere – to want, to crave

damnare – to condemn, damnation

debere – to owe

dementare – destroy one's mind, make someone insane (from the word

mens – *mentis* f. (3) - mind) – dementia

felix – happy

fortis – brave

homini – to a man – Dative case of *homo* – man

ibi – there

inter – between

invidia – *invidiae* f. (3) – envy

iocus – *ioci* m. (2) – joke

egere – to need, to be poor

lavare (1) – to wash – lavatory

magis – more

manus – *manus* f. (4) – hand – manual

medius – middle

mori – to die – moribund

nemo – nobody

nil – nothing

odirit – hates, from *odisse* – to hate – odious

odium – *odii* n. (2) – hatred

ops – *opis* f. (3) – strength, help

parare – to prepare, to raise

prius – first, before, earlier

rasa – erased – from *radere* – to scratch off, to smooth out – razor, eraser

revelare – to reveal

quam – than

quem – whom

sapiens – wise

tempus – time – temporary, temporal

unus – one in number unique

valere – to be well (Vale! – Be well, good bye!

vivere – to live – vivacious

virtus – virtutis f. (3) – virtue, strength

ANSWER KEY – Translation

Lesson I

Esne magister? • Non magister sum. Discipulus sum. • Quid est? Hoc liber est. • Estne stylus? Ita, stylus est. • Estne hoc argentum? Argentum non est. Aurum est. • Estis discipuli/discipulae? Sumus discipuli/discipulae. • Suntne magistri/magistrae? Magistri /magistrae sunt. Estis magistri et discipuli? Magistri non sumus. Discipuli sumus.

silvae et linguae • templa et mercata • argentum et aurum • styli et libri • domini et dominae Estne hoc domus? • Minime, non domus est. Hoc est templum.

Lesson II

Esne tibi nomen Iulius? • Nomen mihi Iulius non est. Nomen mihi Flavius est.• Liber meus bonus est. • Silva magna et mala est. • Estne magister tuus novus bonus? • Liber tuus parvus est. Est mihi liber novus. / Habeo librum novum. • Video amicum novum. – Video amicam novam. Tenet librum magnum. • Magistra tua nova Domina Brown est. • Habeo stylum bonum? Estis magistri mei novi? Magistri tui novi non sumus. Discipuli novi sumus. • Habeo stylum aureum. • Fabula mea vera est. • Fabulae novae bonae sunt.

Lesson III

Lupus rex silvae est. • Amica mea regina terrae magnae est. • gloria Europae • gloria regis carta terrae magnae • rex mundi • liber regis • liber reginae • aqua argentea silvae

Lesson V Translation

Volo in silvis ambulare. • Vult in campis ambulare. • Amat viam longam. Regina florum alborum est. • Leo rex animalium est. • Amo fabulam de avibus albis. Amat fabulam de amicis unicornis. • In insula sum. • In casa sum. • Schola in silva est. Puellae ad scholam ambulant. • Puella tabulam ad scholam portat. • Insulas non amas. schola puellarum

Lesson VII Translation

Ad silvam ambulo. • Ambulas ad silvam, sed ambulo ad mare. • Amo actam. Ambulamus ad actam. • Puellae ad silvam saepe ambulant. • Ad casam ambulamus. Ad casam ambulant. • Ex fenestra spectat. • Patriam amo. • Actam amas sed silvam amo.

Lesson IX Translation

Ubi heri eris? Domi eram. • Et ubi es hodie? Hodie in villa rustica mea sum.

Et ubi cras eris? Cras in urbe eram. • Amici mei in horto heri erant, sed cras in silvis erunt.

Heri magister meus domi erat, sed cras in scholam erit. • Liber lectus est. • Vox regis audita est.

THEATER TERMS

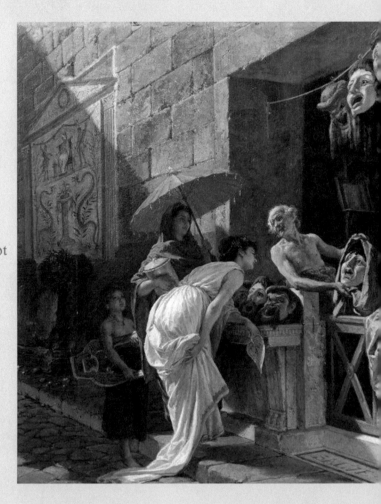

actor << *actor* – performer, plaintiff in court

actress << *actrix* – a female plaintiff

director << *dirigere* – to arrange in line

producer << *producere* – to lead, reveal

script << *scriptum* – written text

stage << *stare* – to stand

intermission << *intermittere* – to interrupt

persona << *persona* – mask

ad lib << *ad libitum* – to one's liking – saying words that are not in the script

amateur << *amare* – to love

audition, auditorium << *audire* – to hear

season<< *satio* – sowing, planting

finale – *finalis* – at the end

admission << *admittere* – to let in

farce << *farcire* – to stuff, to fill up

FASHION /STYLE TERMS

accent << *accentus* – song added to speech

accessory << *accedere* – to approach

antique << *antiquus* – old, ancient

apparel << *ad particulare* – to put together

contrast << *contra + stare* – to stand against

classic << *classicus* – classy, superior

contemporary << *con + tempus*

vintage << *vindemia* – grapes harvest

utilitarian << *utilitas* – usefulness

collection << *collectio* – gathering together

design << *designare* – to mark, to choose

style << *stylus*

elegant << *elegans* – fine, tasteful

fabric << *fabricare* – to make

reversible << *revertere* – to turn back

minimalist << *minimus* – the smallest

retro << *retro* – back, backward

CPSIA information can be obtained
at www.ICGtesting.com
Printed in the USA
LVRC080807171121
703547LV00017BA/91